The INGO Problem

Praise for this book

'*The INGO Problem* is a must-read for international development leaders who have ever wondered how a system that can seem rigid and outdated can better serve civil society. Deborah draws upon her decades of experience to share a critical look at the global INGO landscape and offers an ambitious vision to overcome many of the structural inequities hardwired into the system.'

Darren Walker, OBE, President of the Ford Foundation

'This book is a powerful, timely and brutal critique of how the INGOs show-up in the world. Deborah Doane in this book asks deeply critical but crucial questions of INGOs. I would recommend this book to every person who works with INGOs or inhabits that space, particularly the Boards and leadership of the INGO organisations and spaces. If INGOs want to travel the path of radical transformation for reimagining their future, they would need to earnestly engage with these tough conversations raised in the book.'

Amitabh Behar Acting ED of Oxfam International and former ED of Oxfam India

'This book is a timely reminder that we have waited long enough for the transformative changes we need in how international aid and development are designed and coordinated. Deborah Doane makes a strong call to address barriers that prevent global agencies, governments and donors from delivering on commitments that recognize, enable and resource diverse local civil society groups as key development actors in their own right.'

Lysa John, Secretary-General of CIVICUS

The INGO problem
Power, privilege, and renewal

Deborah Doane

Practical
ACTION
PUBLISHING

Practical Action Publishing Ltd
25 Albert Street, Rugby,
Warwickshire, CV21 2SD, UK
www.practicalactionpublishing.com

A catalogue record for this book is available from the British Library.

A catalogue record for this book has been requested from the Library of Congress.

ISBN 978-1-78853-440-6 Paperback
ISBN 978-1-78853-441-3 Hardback
ISBN 978-1-78853-442-0 Electronic book

Citation: Doane, D., (2024) *The INGO Problem: Power, privilege, and renewal*, Rugby, UK:
Practical Action Publishing http://doi.org/10.3362/9781788534420

Since 1974, Practical Action Publishing has published and disseminated books and
information in support of international development work throughout the world.

Practical Action Publishing is a trading name of Practical Action Publishing Ltd
(Company Reg. No. 1159018), the wholly owned publishing company of Practical
Action. Practical Action Publishing trades only in support of its parent charity
objectives and any profits are covenanted back to Practical Action (Charity Reg. No.
247257, Group VAT Registration No. 880 9924 76).

Cover design by: Michelle Dwyer, Nice & Graphic

Typeset by: Katarzyna Markowska, Practical Action Publishing

Contents

About the author

Deborah Doane has held leadership roles in civil society and philanthropy for over 25 years, across the humanitarian, development, human rights and environment sectors. She is a partner of Rights CoLab and a co-convenor of the RINGO Project, a systems-change initiative to reimagine the international NGO and its relationships in civil society. She writes regularly for the Guardian, Alliance Magazine and other publications about civil society. She is originally from Toronto, Canada but now calls London, UK home.

Foreword

As an organization based in the Global South, the West Africa Civil Society Institute (WACSI), which I currently lead, has experienced the negative impacts of the neocolonial development system and its culture, processes, and practices on multiple occasions. One clear example is a recent experience where WACSI took over a project from a western organization and, in spite of being more experienced and with a proven track record, was taken through a more stringent due diligence process. Examples abound of local organizations openly sharing information with international organizations for joint tender bids but literally being kept in the dark about the process or about other partners' information. These are just a few examples of what organizations that are not just based in but home-grown in the Global South face regularly in their dealings with international organizations.

We were eager, as an organization that supports strengthening civil society primarily in West Africa and the African continent, to see a more equitable system that provides the right environment, resources, and support for civil society, not just in our region, but in Asia and Latin America too. So when Deborah Doane and I met in 2019 as collaborators through Rights CoLab, a virtual organization focusing on human rights and civil society, I was instantly drawn to her enthusiasm for authentically changing the way international development works. And, when Deborah went further and invited me to be a part of a transformative systems change process to fix the broken international development system, specifically by reimagining the role of one of its key actors, the INGO, I readily said 'yes'. The idea of transforming the international development system was not new, but what set her work apart was her determination to take action rather than just discussing it. This made a significant impact on me personally and organizationally.

Thus, my colleagues and I at WACSI joined forces with other colleagues to advance the Reimagining the INGO (RINGO) agenda. This book, borne out of that process, reflects the collective efforts of a dedicated and passionate global community of international development changemakers.

With the current discourse on decolonization, localization, and shifting power in the international development space, this book arrives at the perfect time. Organizations and individuals active in this field struggle to understand and apply these concepts, and to bring about transformative change that could impact them personally. As a trustee of Oxfam Great Britain, I have first-hand experience and knowledge of the challenges (both internally and externally) that organizations like Oxfam face and the commitments that they have made to decolonization in word and in deed. In spite of the challenges there is a determination to forge ahead on the journey of transformation.

At the same time, the often-neglected contribution of actors in the global majority, who are really the front liners and who bring so much value to the table, are not recognized in the current system. The INGO problem is one that cannot be solved by INGOs alone and needs the inclusion of actors in the global majority who are often marginalized and not part of the decision-making in the international development space, yet are the supposed recipients of development. This is a yarn that is spun without their involvement and thrust upon them, whether it fits or not. The immense potential for global development that meaningfully includes truly global actors from different parts of the globe who understand their contexts and should lead in finding the solutions to their development problems is a key part of fixing the broken system. Let s/he who has ears hear what needs to be heard and acted upon.

Deborah offers practical solutions for achieving real transformation whilst providing clarity on complex issues and concepts. She assesses the sector honestly and comprehensively, particularly INGOs, highlighting both flaws and progressive aspects. She skilfully weaves together narratives of RINGO prototypes and their contributions to solving sector problems. Furthermore, citing first-hand accounts from key actors in their fields, she highlights other initiatives that are working to fix the broken system, ranging from individual organizations and consortia to movements like #ShiftThePower.

Deborah has a deep understanding of the sector from its very core. From her initial idealistic expectations as a development studies graduate to the realities and disappointments she encountered while navigating different constituencies in the sector, she takes us on a personal journey that is intimately connected to systemic issues. She is both self-reflective and insightful in her examination of external factors and in her 'take no prisoners' scrutiny of the work of INGOs and how it can be improved to create a more equitable, just, and fair international development system. She explores systemic blockages, such as risk and compliance, paternalistic/patronizing partnerships, accountability, language, storytelling, and governance. These challenges, she emphasizes, affect all different groups, including those focused on human rights, humanitarian aid, peacebuilding, development, the environment, and more. The need for system-wide change is clear, and everyone has a role to play.

This book embraces authenticity and balance by acknowledging both the negative aspects of the current system and the positive ones. Importantly, it avoids being caught up in over-analysis; instead, it suggests a way forward with practical examples of past, ongoing, and potential actions. It explores the role that INGOs play in an outdated system and why that role is no longer adequate.

While the journey ahead will not be easy for those in the international system, there is a way forward that is both constructive and hopeful. With *The INGO Problem*, Deborah proves that, with the right support, our sector – both actors in INGOs and the global majority – have a promising future.

Nana Asantewa Afadzinu

Introduction

This book is, above all, a personal reflection on the international non-governmental organization (INGO) sector and how it needs to transform itself in order to play a more constructive role as part of global civil society. While there have been many things to applaud about INGOs historically, as will be revealed throughout the book, the INGO – once a model of an ethical civil society sector trying to provide resilience and hope to many in the world – is being challenged on all sides, both internally and externally. Internally, the sector faces challenges in response to a series of scandals in recent years around racism and sexual exploitation. There have also been louder and louder demands to 'decolonize' and shift power to local organizations. The sector faces challenges from funders wanting them to be more 'accountable' – or worse, no longer wanting to fund them at all – as funders in turn face demands to spend more funding locally.[1] There is even 'competition' from the private sector, which has moved into the civil society space and captured millions in government funding. Externally, the sector is facing up to the fact that it will never be the pillar to solving some of the biggest challenges of our time, as it once claimed to be, with many issues, such as the climate crisis and growing conflicts, getting worse rather than better in recent years.

While I use this space to share my own observations and deeper analysis based on over 25 years' experience in civil society, the book draws heavily on the work of the RINGO Project and its many participants, some of whom were interviewed for the preparation of this book. RINGO is a systems-change initiative to re-imagine the INGO, which was started in late 2020 by myself and some colleagues around the world. RINGO was, first and foremost, built out of our strong alliance with the #ShiftThePower movement, a collective of civil society organizations (CSOs) and community philanthropy groups that argue in favour of stronger national and local civil societies and more democratic and inclusive forms of engagement. In my first introduction to the movement, I heard about the multiple concerns of local civil society actors who felt that INGOs were consistently taking away their oxygen – in terms of money, power, and voice – rather than adding value to their work.[2] My anecdotal findings were later backed up by research undertaken by academics, other CSOs, as well as the West Africa Civil Society Institute, a collaborator of the Ringo Project.

RINGO initially gathered 50 people who represented the system, and a wider engaged community of roughly 1,000 people, over a 2-year period of intense reflection and action from 2021 to 2023, continuing to the present (early 2024, at time of writing). During the initial phase of the work, we explored why the system wasn't working for the majority in civil society, especially those at the local level. We addressed questions throughout the project around power and trust; diversity and racism; governance and accountability; funding and ownership; culture and more. As a response, we launched a series of 'prototypes' to help re-imagine the system. Many of these prototypes – and the stories that led to their creation – are discussed in this book, and some are starting to be embedded in the civil society ecosystem.

RINGO wasn't anti-INGO, but it was certainly challenging the dominance of the sector in its current incarnation. Although we need a form of global civil society in which different groups and aspirations can be connected and supported, the INGO model we have, the one that evolved over the past few decades, is no longer fit for purpose. It needs to cede space to others, and find a new role and purpose, if it is to add value towards solving seemingly intractable problems, from the climate crisis to inequality to human rights. As part of the community of social change actors, from social movements to political parties, INGOs' role is skewed: they take the bulk of civil society funding, resource, and visibility, in a context where other civil society actors do the bulk of the work.

Many of the long-standing INGOs are acutely aware of the challenges they face, and there have been several efforts by international CSOs and their respective networks to address the critiques. Some of these efforts include decentralizing organizations and rethinking the country office model, addressing safeguarding issues, and developing more participatory funding mechanisms, alongside a myriad of collective initiatives across the sector. However, these responses are yet to revolutionize the international civil society sector. Instead, many have proven to be technocratic responses to more fundamental and political challenges, or simply talk shops. RINGO was initiated to overturn the sense of inertia that prevails, and to find new ways to shift power to national and local civil societies, while also designing the INGO we ultimately want and need.

The book isn't intended to be a full blueprint for a model INGO but instead shows how both small and larger practical changes in the way we organize and work in civil society can deliver a more fair and equitable civil society. The first chapter gives a brief potted history of INGOs, situating my own personal experience within this. The remaining chapters focus on the things that need changing, drawing on the experience of others working in both civil society and philanthropy, as well as that of the RINGO Project. Chapter 2 outlines a renewed purpose for INGOs – one based in a supportive role, rather than in the driver's seat. Chapter 3 takes a deeper look into structure and governance, sign-posting some opportunities for transformation. Risk management and accountability, which are some of the foundations of formal CSOs, are exposed and given an overhaul in Chapter 4. In Chapter 5, I turn to the funders of the sector, including philanthropists and governments, but including INGOs as funders too – discussion of the latter being something that I think has been seriously lacking in the discourse around the sector. Chapter 6 explores issues of language and culture, in an attempt to get into some of the more underlying and structural challenges we need to address. Chapter 7 takes a closer look at some of the different and distinct INGO sectors: the humanitarian sector, development, environment, human rights, and peacebuilding. And finally, in Chapter 8, I suggest some ways forward. The story is, of course, constantly evolving, both as I write and as you read. None of this will ever be complete, but it's a start.

My hope is that, with the ideas and stories that emerge throughout, those who are in positions to change their own institutions – through collaboration and radical transformation – can find the drive to do so, and that the debate that has been brewing for some years will enable people to move from thought to action. A key dimension that must be recognized, though, is that, while individual institutions can instigate some of this shift, it takes many individuals, organizations and institutions to transform the sector. These need to represent all parts of the ecosystem to really bring about collective change: funders, INGOs, regulators, and others. All of the stakeholders are addressed at some point in this book, and I offer both explicit and implicit ideas about their roles.

I hope the book arms people with sufficient anger at the current system, but also with enough inspiration to do something – ideally in equal measure. From my own experience in campaigning and social change, a bit of anger is a helpful spark to action. There is also some comfort in the fact that 'you're not alone' in thinking the system isn't quite working as it should do, but that doesn't mean you should abandon all hope. There is *always* something you can do, whatever role you might play in the system, whether you're a young recruit, a veteran working in a local NGO, a board member of an INGO, or a funder. If we didn't believe that change was always possible, I suspect none of us would even be affiliated with civil society in the first place.

And finally, while the critiques may seem harsh at times, I am still, and will always be, a passionate believer in civil society as a force for good in the world: we just need our major institutions to contribute in a way that reinforces that. The world, with all of its many challenges, absolutely needs civil society, so let's make it work better for all of us, wherever we may be.

CHAPTER ONE
Times they are a-changin'

When I started working in the INGO sector, I came into it wide-eyed and hopeful. It was a second career for me, having started out as a civil servant in the Canadian government as a 'policy analyst' – a generic term that saw me working on everything from health policy to federal government devolution to the Inuit-led territory of Nunavut in the Canadian Arctic. But I was restless and wanted to go beyond my country to see what else was out there, so I embarked on a new adventure. This was the mid-1990s, and I was in my late 20s.

Like many people who work in the sector, I started with a Master's degree in Development Studies. At the time, the idea of development work rang of intelligent altruism, with the laudable aim of helping 'poor people' (a phrase I now rabidly avoid). I, with my privilege and experience in public service, could go deeper, do more. We learned about economics, about the difference between 'least developed countries' and emerging economies, and about the challenges of bringing 'capitalism' to countries without democracy; we learned about conflict and humanitarianism; our minds were opened to issues around how to manage the commons, and to participatory development. After a sweeping year of indoctrination, we could now go out into the world and practise 'development'. We were an international cohort, from Colombia, Nigeria, the Philippines, the US, Italy, India, and beyond. Armed with a year of 'expertise', some went on to work for the World Bank or the International Labour Organization; others for their governments, as diplomats and senior civil servants; one person went on to advise poorer countries' finance departments, including Papua New Guinea, through high-level internships affiliated with northern-led think tanks. A few sought PhDs and many years later went onto run INGOs themselves or to teach the next generation.

Thanks to a kindly academic, and some clear privilege, I, with zero humanitarian experience, was drafted in to work on what was known as the 'Ombudsman Project', a response to the failings of the aid sector during the 1994 Rwandan genocide, coordinated on behalf of the sector by the British Red Cross. The project sought to set up an accountability mechanism for actors working in humanitarian aid. At the time, an evaluation report came out by academics at the Overseas Development Institute, a large British development think tank, that unpacked the humanitarian effort in Rwanda and its commensurate failings.[3] The evaluation was highly critical of the international community's response to the genocide, one that ultimately led to the death of an estimated 800,000 people over 100 days. Political action, including from the United Nations (UN), was slow and ineffective, so humanitarian agencies, already on the scene, became the front-face of the response to the tragedy that emerged.

But far from being considered a humanitarian success, the crisis shone a spotlight on the INGO sector's structural failings: from lack of coordination to brand competition, lack of accountability, and an absence of adequate standards. This paved the way for multiple attempts to improve the sector ever since, including the Ombudsman Project.

During my three years with the project, I had an induction into the sector that very quickly took the shine off my then-chosen career path. It may have been the first INGO-branded fleet I saw, which seemed to lord its way over Kigali, or perhaps it was the head of emergencies at a well-known aid agency who said to me when I asked for a job, 'I only want staff working for us who "bleed" [insert brand name] when we cut them open'.

Whatever the trigger (and there were many), I very quickly knew that I didn't want to join the ranks of people who flew around the world moving from one refugee camp to another, trying to 'save' people. Although many were kind and deeply engaged, a vast cohort was also arrogant, patronizing and self-important. The overwhelming sense of superiority and power didn't sit well with my middle-class, fair-minded Canadian sensibilities. I realized that I wasn't altruistically trying to help the poor; instead I was underpinning an industry that often seemed to be exploiting, rather than helping. I quickly moved on.

In the years that followed, as I watched from the margins of the sector, multiple INGO failures and scandals have hit the headlines. Yet in spite of these headlines, the institution still seems to prevail, and INGOs have continued to play a dominant role in the international civil society system, the brands growing ever larger, with outsized influence to match. Some of the incomes of the organizations are now staggering, with several now reaching the US$1 or $2 billion mark, their CEOs, including former British Foreign Secretary, David Miliband, earning well over $1 million per year.

What remains the same since I first joined the sector over 25 years ago is that, despite some of the sector-wide responses to scandals, reviews, or evaluations, INGOs remain largely unaccountable – except to their donors and, perhaps, to the media. The very people that the Ombudsman Project in the late 1990s was aiming to serve continue to be an afterthought.

What has changed, however, is that now, finally, INGOs are facing a reckoning. They are being challenged both from outside and within. There are the not-so-surprising anti-democratic populists, who scapegoat civil society, including INGOs, in order to stem opposition. But more surprisingly, critiques have also come from within civil society itself, generally from those situated in places INGOs are meant to be serving: Africa, Asia, and Latin America. A movement, under the auspices of #ShiftThePower, is generating force, not just targeting the failings of the sector and asking for it to do a *little bit better*; but rather demanding a complete overhaul of how we organize global civil society and the wider aid system as a whole.

Many of my colleagues from the 1990s who remained working in the sector are now peering into the mirror and reflecting on their life's work; some are walking away, while others are staying the course to try to change the sector from within. But among so many of us there is a feeling of discomfort at the sector's standing: over the years, it has come out in the quiet whisper at the pub or the cynical side-glance in a meeting. More recently, it's the private message during a larger Zoom call discussion, or the WhatsApp message saying 'can we speak?'

The good news is that we don't need to keep these things to ourselves any more: the movement is growing and we can all be part of it. We can start to generate and share our stories of change and possibility: stories of giving up power or walking in solidarity. Moreover, we can take action and do something about it, rather than living with the status quo.

As the familiar Bob Dylan song goes, 'times, they are a-changin''.

Who do you trust?

The Edelman Trust Barometer is a pretty good indicator of which institutions people trust in society. Public relations company Edelman regularly surveys thousands of people around the world about their trust in business, government, media, and NGOs.[4]

In 2003, NGOs were considered the most trusted type of institution across the US, UK, and Europe. Even the least trusted NGO ranked among the highest trusted corporate brands. The top INGO brands, far outranking the corporate sector, included the likes of the World Wide Fund for Nature (WWF), Amnesty International, Oxfam, and Greenpeace.

Fast forward to 2023, and trust in NGOs is not just falling in these countries, it is now below many of those in the corporate sector, and has fallen more than any other sector surveyed in most countries. How did we get here in such a short space of time?

International NGOs have been stricken by some damning scandals since Edelman's 'peak trust' reading in 2003. The chinks in the armour seemed to come when scandals hit the headlines: a significant *New Yorker* essay from 2010, for one, charged the humanitarian sector with aiding and abetting conflicts;[5] after the Haiti earthquake in 2010, which saw a huge outpouring of public sympathy, it was revealed that very little of the money actually made it to local people;[6] not long after, in the UK, fundraising scandals hit the headlines, showing egregious fundraising practices, particularly targeting older people. This was followed by the safeguarding scandals in 2018 that uncovered historic cases of sexual abuse by staff in organizations including well-known mainstays, such as Oxfam, Save the Children, and the Red Cross, leading to a huge global outcry, with shocking headlines like 'Oxfam's deputy CEO resigns over sex crime scandal'.[7] Over the years, many books and essays have been written by sector experts, journalists, and academics, all crying out about the hypocrisies in the sector, and the need for it to transform.

Wrongdoing in INGOs holds a larger sway over people's feelings about them than those from other sectors. Perhaps unlike the corporate sector or even the government, where scandals are commonplace, we expect them to only do good things, not harmful ones. 'In our pursuit of doing good, we've also done harm. That's one of the hardest things to understand. We've always thought of ourselves as the better angels of our nature. That's difficult for people to get their head around', says Dylan Mathews, the Chief Executive of Peace Direct.

The scandals are also magnified by external political forces, with populists using these failings to advance their own agendas: placing blame on civil society when things go wrong, declaring them the enemy of development, or even democracy, in a trend known as 'closing civic space'. In recent years, closing civic space has seen large organizations, such as Amnesty International, Greenpeace, and Action Aid, being attacked and maligned and kicked out of countries altogether. This plays into the narrative that they are no longer institutions we can trust.

There is a further hypothesis that bears thinking about: that INGOs are vulnerable to critiques for a more existential reason. Indeed, the failings and attacks on INGOs are part of a deeper malaise and flaw in the origins and institutional design of the INGO itself, one that finds itself wrapped up in neocolonial undertones that, if not reconciled, will spell out its death sooner rather than later. Author Barney Tallack, for one, argues that 'INGOs will either have to transform, die well or die badly'.[8]

The importance of history to the INGO project

The origins of INGOs can be traced back to the founding of the International Red Cross movement in the 1860s, established to provide relief during times of war and natural disasters. Humanitarian relief by INGOs expanded significantly during the Second World War, when NGOs helped to provide relief and assistance to civilians, either through solidarity or hands-on support. Organizations like Oxfam, Catholic Relief Services, Plan, and CARE International all emerged during this time. Many INGOs gained their first glimpse of political standing with the creation of the UN's Economic and Social Council, (ECOSOC) in which 40 INGOs received 'consultative' status, in 1946, ensuring they were already fully embedded in influencing discussions with UN bodies and national governments.

The period of self-determination of many countries in Africa and South America in the 1960s coincided with the arrival of the 'development agenda'. INGOs proliferated during this time, in a second period of expansion, especially in former colonized countries across Africa. Colonial rulers stepped back, and some countries entered into what academic Mark Duffield described as a 'permanent emergency',[9] where governments themselves, either new or former colonial governments, were unable to respond to the needs of populations caught in the aftermath of colonization. INGOs grew during this time and, in effect, became de facto new colonizers themselves, setting up offices to supplant the role of state services, from education to healthcare, fuelled by people in the west opening their pockets and passing their money on, embedding the view that would perpetuate the image of countries unable to help themselves or solve their own problems. More and more humanitarian and development organizations entered the fray: Médecins Sans Frontières, Action Against Hunger, and Mercy Corps, for example.

The 1960s and 1970s also saw a rise in INGOs representing other issues, responding to human rights, or environmental concerns: Greenpeace and WWF in the environment space; Amnesty International and Human Rights Watch in the human rights sphere. Some started strictly at a national level, like the Nature Conservancy in the US in the 1950s, which only expanded internationally from the 1970s onwards. This presented a new opportunity for western-led INGOs to dominate thinking and influencing on the political stage, across a whole new set of issues.

Anyone who grew up in the 1980s will have a vivid memory of Bob Geldof's Live Aid concert in 1984, following on the heels of his immensely successful song 'Do They Know It's Christmas?', which saw millions and millions of dollars pouring into INGOs to save the victims of the Ethiopian famine. Starving black babies flashed across our television screens, interspersed with a catchy tune. Geldof raised the money – INGOs were the vehicle for spending it.

The time sowed the seeds for an emerging clash between civil and political rights versus economic and social rights that plays out today; at the same time western-led INGOs were waving the flag for civil and political rights. Western governments were using civil and political rights as bargaining chips in the aid game, often forgoing the former in favour of the latter, especially in exchange for political alliances along Cold War lines.[10] Structural adjustment policies, which imposed western free-market economic models on lower-income countries, made many countries even poorer, opening the door for further economic colonization by the richer countries of the world. Investment in development from Organisation for Economic Co-operation and Development (OECD) governments grew, partly delivered through the INGO sector, as long as it remained neutral and charitable. They talked about human rights, but quietly evaded its enforcement.

After a few decades in trying to achieve poverty relief, it was clear that charity wasn't going to solve the problems of the world. Economic justice concerns finally came to the fore in the 1980s and 1990s, responding to the structural adjustment policies of the World Bank and the International Monetary Fund, which ultimately indebted so many countries, requiring them to adopt capitalist policies and open markets that made many poorer, not richer. This gave rise to a wider (and perhaps welcome) remit for many development INGOs, who now took to looking at root causes with more depth, with some focusing on issues such as international debt relief and government accountability. Organizations like CARE and Oxfam took on a more political face and grew their advocacy arms, while new groups like Transparency International entered the fore, seeking to call out corruption and hold governments to account. Some groups, like the Jubilee Debt Campaign, took on a more movement-based approach, developing their work from the grassroots upwards, but most retained a traditional, western-led model of the INGO.

Even with a growing number of national offices of INGOs being established, the work continued to be led by those with power and resource rooted firmly in Europe or the US. Philanthropy, government funding, and an army of fundraising experts provided the investment needed to enable INGOs' offices and jobs to proliferate around the world. Northern (usually white) staff members would take the helm in such 'field' postings, often on salaries that were far larger than those of their local counterparts.

Through the chorus of northern-led INGOs and well-resourced think tanks advising governments, even being the loudest voices in protest, western knowledge and western influence on the international stage was secured. Fast forward to the 2020s and you can find western-led INGOs in every corner of the world and in every space of social change, operating across a multitude of specialist issues – older people, peacebuilding, young people, trade justice, and disabled people, to name a few – alongside multiple faith-based groups, representing Christian faiths, Muslim faiths, and Judaism. And many, many more.

All of these seeds have one thing in common: they began with people from the rich world's concern for people and issues in poorer parts of the world – offering a genuine desire to help where, often, governments and the political system had failed. Conflict, famine, human rights, or environmental degradation were the catalysts for people to come together to find civic solutions or to broaden political support for those most in need.

With significant influence, and considerable resource, many INGOs have done a stellar job of raising the stakes on global issues, from inequality to climate change. A global deal reached in 2004, pushed by major INGOs at the G7, helped to secure international debt relief for 27 countries, valued at over US$70 billion.[11] Environmental INGOs helped to secure the lauded UN Ocean Treaty, adopted in 2023, considered a global breakthrough in marine conservation.[12] INGOs have provided a unique watchdog function, coalescing citizen concerns into messages and actions, holding companies and governments alike to account. And, of course, many have delivered much-needed help in times of need when the world's governments and political systems have failed.

When I set up the Corporate Responsibility (CORE) coalition in the early 2000s to tackle corporate power, larger professionalized civil society groups helped to lay the foundation for a successful campaign: Action Aid, Christian Aid, WWF, Amnesty International, and others were all involved. They brought capacity to research, opened doors to corporate power holders in the City of London, the centre of the UK's finance sector, and with politicians alike; and had the 'muscle' to get coverage in the media, while mobilizing their membership base. At one point we were able to claim 7 million supporters for our cause. Collectively, we achieved, at the time, groundbreaking changes to UK company law that has an impact to this day. For me, this was the pinnacle of good-INGO-dom.

Yet over time, the star has slipped away, whether as a result of scandals or scapegoating – or both. Moreover, the original simple charitable or solidaristic endeavours, like Oxfam providing food parcels or the Amnesty model of trying to get political prisoners released, evolved into hugely complex and hungry organizations, competing for resources and brand and identity. Far from being rooted in voluntarism, they become professionalized entities, the corporate behemoth of civil society, all with lofty ambitions to either 'end poverty', 'end war', 'save the planet', or 'protect human rights'.

The problem is, they haven't, nor can they.

The tide turns

In 1992, political philosopher Francis Fukuyama released a seminal book declaring the 'end of history'.[13] He argued that neo-liberal democracy had trumped all other political forms and would drive higher standards of living as a fait accompli. Open markets, alongside basic democracy, and a strong civil society, were thus the cornerstones of the future.

INGOs themselves were, for the most part, caught up in this consensus, and accepted most, if not all, of this hypothesis. Even when fighting for things like trade justice, as they did en masse at the standout World Trade Organization protests in Seattle in 1999, they were working with the tide of neo-liberalism and not against it.[14] While some social movements and smaller INGOs were firmly in the 'end capitalism' camp, INGOs navigated the middle ground: calling on corporations to behave fairly vis-à-vis creating new social or environmental standards, and taking funds from governments and the corporate sector to continue their 'important', expansive work. Some more radical groups called out corporations' funding of charities as 'greenwashing', but the INGOs were largely immune to this call as the incomes of the big players rose and organizations got ever larger, with more and more brand presence across the globe. Pandas (WWF's logo) were stamped on everything from furniture to bank cards, as 'affinity products' became a staple diet of fundraising departments everywhere. Companies happily partnered with the INGO sector to keep customers and build their brand's fuzzy feeling, as a shield against criticism.

In this foray, the reality of what had really happened in civil society passed many INGOs by. Almost immediately after 9/11, civil society was reframed as a centre of suspicion and distrust in almost all corners of the globe. INGOs may not have been entirely oblivious to growing populism and a breaking down of the neo-liberal consensus that acted in some ways as their armour, but they were certainly on the back foot: repressive governments backlashed against them, as happened in Turkey, India, and Nicaragua. INGOs were no longer the good guys: they were the enemy. And not just of states: of other actors in civil society too. Countries immediately imposed banking restrictions and anti-terrorism laws that were weaponized against NGOs, accusing them of fomenting dissent. They divided civil society actors between the 'knitters' (providing basic charity) and the 'trouble makers' (those fighting for human rights or social justice). A chill fell across the world, impacting so many civil society groups.[15]

Despite the growing set of restrictions, by 2016 civil society groups in the majority world – Africa, Latin America, the Middle East, and Asia – were calling for more political responsiveness beyond the few scraps of neo-liberal 'development'. And importantly, in some corners, they saw INGOs as part of the problem, not part of the solution. The first gathering inklings of the backlash came to the fore that year in Johannesburg, where local civil society organizations coalesced around a nascent hashtag, #ShiftThePower.[16] They identified a set of challenges and behaviours that INGOs and funders alike were exhibiting that inhibited their own growth, capacity, and impact. It took a few years for the wave to really hit shore.[17]

By the time the Black Lives Matter movement rose to the international stage in the early days of the COVID-19 pandemic, there was a strong call for INGOs to confront their own racism and decolonize themselves. It was a clear moment of reckoning, unleashing a voice that had been quietly growing from within. The problem of the 'white saviour' started to be discussed in more mainstream spaces. There was increasing realization that INGOs received a disproportionate share of resources; that white people got all the high-paid jobs and made most of the decisions; and that they acted like distant middle-men, exploiting those at the bottom.

To some observers, INGOs are now as far removed from the concept of civil society as most people in local communities could begin to imagine. Engaging with an INGO seems, at times, more akin to asking a bank for money than sitting down in solidarity to solve a problem.

Today, a stronger and more united voice than the quiet whisper down the pub is calling for real and dramatic change. It says that civil society is needed, but not necessarily the one we have now, as represented by the institution of the INGO. History has changed and moved on – and certainly not ended – but INGOs haven't moved with it. Until now. The tide seems to have finally turned. A quick trawl of events on 'decolonization' of civil society or philanthropy in the months of August and September 2023 showed no fewer than 15 events looking at everything from shifting power to decolonizing: training courses, talks, and webinars, some hosted by people in Europe or North America, others led by people in Africa and Asia.

***

The unending rise of INGOs has most certainly had its day. But this isn't to say that INGOs are wholly redundant either. As we explore throughout this book, even with a revolution from other civil society actors demanding transformation, there are renewed roles and opportunities for INGOs.

And we all have a role to play in driving change: board members, leaders, public donors, funders, academics, and partners alike. We need to keep the demand for change high on the agenda and not complacently cling to the models that have dominated, because it's just too hard to change. INGOs will never be the ones to solve poverty or the climate crisis, or end conflict or discrimination, so let's let go of that illusion before we go any further.

There are signs of light, with some wonderful examples emerging that have begun to shift the dial, at least in part – such as the Australian Red Cross, which fully re-designed its operating model in 2019, and moved away from direct implementation, shifting to multi-year core funding to local partners.[18] Or indeed, the many signatories to the Pledge for Change, a collaborative initiative of INGOs, such as CARE and Oxfam, to decolonize their own practice. But those pushing for change within the sector continue to face huge barriers to change, and even with all of this talk of change, still don't occupy mainstream practice. In this book, I explore some of the barriers and propose how we might work together to see the new practices become the overwhelming norm in our relationships in international civil society and cement a clear renewed role and purpose for INGOs.

INGOs remain an important vehicle for bringing people together, for democracy and beyond. To fulfil this potential, they must let go of their colonial roots, and of the quiet alliance with the underpinnings of neo-liberal economics. If we go forward with humility and understanding, INGOs can finally move with the changing times.

CHAPTER TWO
The purpose and role of INGOs

In August 2022, a group of Ukrainian civil society organizations (CSOs) wrote an open letter[19] to INGOs telling them what they wanted and needed from them. This was six months into the war in Ukraine. Just after the war started, many INGOs with a development background launched appeals to help the victims of war. The appeal by the Disasters Emergency Committee in the UK — a collaboration of the largest humanitarian agencies — raised over £50 million in its first weekend alone.[20] By the time the letter was issued, INGOs had raised millions all over the world to support people in Ukraine. Governments had also contributed, mainly to United Nations (UN) agencies that subcontracted to INGOs. Yet by August, very few local organizations had seen any of this funding, and so the local organizations finally took a public stand. An appeal from local organizations was initiated.

Most of the INGOs who launched appeals didn't have existing relationships with organizations in Ukraine — or anywhere in Eastern Europe, for that matter. Their traditional stomping grounds were Africa, South Asia, or Latin America. They scrambled to get staff out there, make connections, and do 'needs assessments' of local organizations. Local CSOs, who were already very active in providing on-the-spot support, found they had to prove their credibility – one local CSO reported that they had to fill out 36 forms to become a 'trusted partner' of an international agency. They had to meet and greet the likes of Médecins Sans Frontières (MSF), Oxfam, and Save the Children and repeat their 'needs' time and time again, until any sort of coordination mechanism was in place (and in some cases, in spite of there being one). Their own staff and volunteers continued to provide help on the ground, and did so for months without resources, risking their health and their lives in the process.

In the end, most INGOs concluded that there was little they could do inside Ukraine. They were outside of their context and their systems didn't allow for money to easily get to those on the ground who needed it. Most had to figure out what to do with the millions raised for the humanitarian effort, often offering little more than food or clothing parcels at the borders. Some channelled funds for 'capacity building', implying local organizations had no idea what they were doing, or that they needed to build up their capacity for form-filling and upwards accountability.

The Ukrainian CSOs, instead, appealed for solidarity. They wanted INGOs to be in service to their needs, to cut bureaucracy and recognize that the situation was fast-moving and that local people were much better at understanding what was needed, and how it should be delivered. Moreover, they didn't want INGOs representing them and speaking on their behalf – they wanted their own channels to communicate and appeal to the international community and even the general public.

It wasn't the first letter of its kind — a more general one appeared on openDemocracy[21] in 2020 from national and sub-national civil society groups, calling out INGO attempts to 'localise', a trend that has grown significantly in recent years. This letter had a more acerbic tone to it and on reading one senses a huge eye-rolling from the anonymous authors and signatories, as in 'I can't believe we're still facing this *%$@ nonsense!'. 'Do you need to exist in every country with your brand? No. There are often local organisations, like ourselves, who work effectively on the ground, with better connections to the local community. And many of us also have the skills and capacity to represent our issues on the world stage,' they write.

The Ukrainian letter served as a reminder, just two years later, and in the midst of a major global crisis, of how little INGOs are able to adapt and learn. Multiple evaluations of INGO interventions, especially in the emergency context, have highlighted similar issues for decades, including in the responses to the Haitian earthquake in 2010, the Asian tsunami in 2004, and the Rwandan genocide in 1994. All of these evaluations cite the imposition of large agencies from the outside coming in, implying they have more knowledge and skills (and thereby using their access to international resources to override local actors), lacking coordination, and generally leaving people bereft of resources and excluded from being agents of their own development.

Is this what most INGOs want to see? Probably not. But the condition seems baked into the system: this is the role and purpose of the INGO as it has evolved over the last few decades. The role and the purpose of the INGO needs a revisit – and a serious change of direction.

Who do we think we are?

You don't have to look too far to find out how INGOs currently portray their assumed role in the world. A simple trawl of websites reveals quite a lot about how they see their place – usually as conduits of hope that the world's problems can be solved through their lens. There is a sense that if only we put our attention to things through supporting a particular INGO, the seemingly insurmountable problem can be solved:

> 'We are Oxfam: Let's beat poverty together.' – Oxfam GB

> 'We are campaigning for a world where human rights are enjoyed by all … No government is beyond scrutiny. No situation is beyond hope.' – Amnesty International

> 'Peace is within our power.' – International Alert

> 'We are ending violence and fighting poverty so that all women, everywhere, can create the future they want.' – Action Aid

Taken on their own, these statements are important signposts to engage people, a motivating call-to-arms. When the charity fundraisers on street corners (known as 'chuggers') approach you to sign up for a direct debit, it's these inspiring words that draw you in. The world seems to be falling apart; *this* is something I can do.

I don't disagree that civil society *does* have a critical role to play in solving some of today's problems, and that we need people to have a sense of belief in the possible. But dig a little deeper and this overarching message, which is the front-face greeting of many INGOs, also goes beyond a mere aspiration to frame the role they want to play: one of Machiavellian splendour, armed with resources and solutions if only people would open their cheque books and listen.

Consider another lens: at least two decades ago, INGOs took a strong liking to private-sector consultancy McKinsey-style management techniques, as part of the move towards professionalization of the sector. Now, most INGOs have a vision, mission, and strategy statement that creates an overarching layer to help define their purpose and lead their strategic approach.

'Our mission is to break cycles of violence and to build sustainable peace.' – International Alert

'CARE International works around the globe to save lives, defeat poverty, and achieve social justice.' – CARE International

'Our mission is to build a future in which people live in harmony with nature.' – World Wide Fund for Nature

The ambitions are set high and the words are compelling, addictive, and heartfelt. They serve the purpose of generating that much-needed support – financial or otherwise – for the cause at hand. Nobody really challenges these words, framings, or aspirations. They have become, in effect, the conduits for many progressive dreams and hopes, where our political system has failed to deliver. The danger is that they are ultimately rendered meaningless. INGOs give the impression of success, where feeding the beast becomes a purpose in itself – a business rather than an altruistic force. As Danny Sriskandarajah, former CEO of Oxfam GB, says:

If you are successful, say, raising 100 million pounds a year through your shops and another 100 million in public fundraising, that's amazing. But soon you start building up fixed costs – from staff in the UK to country offices to fleets of cars – and you become protective, and as costs rise, you have to work harder to raise more income. So success can end up breeding risk aversion and control freakery.

Gatekeepers and power brokers

For at least a few decades now, INGOs have unquestioningly assumed the role of global watchdog and progressive champion, with every international political gathering, from the G20, to

Davos, to major UN summits, accompanied by a cohort of INGOs on their tail, lobbying, making noise, and hoping to influence outcomes. In these hallowed halls, they represent 'the voices of the excluded' carrying the weight of champion of the poor on their heavy shoulders.

But they've also played a Janus-faced role: calling out governments on the one hand, while assuming the role of contractor to government on the other. Most humanitarian emergencies, for one, see large sums of money being channelled through INGOs to deliver services. Governments, meanwhile, see them as an efficient means of moving money and doing their bidding. It's in this latter role that INGOs most often come in for criticism by despotic regimes and activists alike. It's the combination of these two roles that makes the INGO perhaps more powerful on paper than it would otherwise seem if you were just looking at the balance sheet alone. INGOs have consciously hardwired their purpose and role into the international political system, making them necessary agents to engage with for local civil society actors who want access to resources or to the international political system. In other words, they have evolved from providing solidaristic support to become the gatekeepers for both influence and funding in the civil society system almost everywhere they operate.

Want to influence a Conference of Parties (COP) on climate change? You need an INGO partner. Are you a local organization who needs money to support people in a conflict? You need an INGO partner. Want to alert a donor government that their trade policies are causing harm to the poorest in your country? Let an INGO represent you. Are you a government who needs to give away aid? More 'efficient' to do so through an INGO. Want to ensure local CSOs are accountable for their funding? An INGO can do the checks for you.

And it's this role and purpose that is the root of the problem that so many local CSOs are starting to push back against. If the words in the mission statements were written with less hyperbole, and a dose of realism, they might instead read like this: 'we use your money to employ quite a lot of white people in London/Washington/Geneva to do some amount of good, but not much money will make it to where you think it's intended, and also we can't guarantee things will actually be better after we've spent your money. But we'll try to do what we can, within the confines of charity law/government contractual obligations'.

What do we want? Equity! When do we want it? Now!

In late 2020, the West Africa Civil Society Institute (WACSI), as part of the RINGO Project, conducted a public survey[22] of local CSOs' experiences with INGOs and what they wanted to happen. The starkest insight that came out of that survey was the fact that while over 84% of the over 600 respondents said they have collaborations with INGOs, 85% of these did not find the relationship to be mutually beneficial: the practices and structures didn't acknowledge local realities and were based on western-defined norms and expectations. Many were seen as effectively subcontractors to INGOs: strategies were defined in the INGO offices and the national or local CSOs were expected to implement projects and programmes accordingly.

Less than a year after the Ukrainian letter was written, a group of Polish organizations supporting the millions of migrants displaced as a result of the war penned their own open letter, in response to the ongoing frustrations they too were experiencing working with the international sector. They called out the role that was allocated to them as 'implementing partner', a paternalistic slight that means they implement the INGO or UN vision. Instead, they appealed for an equal partnership in the endeavour.[23]

Like the Ukrainian organizations, the Polish organizations wrote about the problems of bureaucracy and how it takes their time away from helping people, the ridiculous amounts of form-filling and meetings, and the expectations to keep all INGOs informed of all of their work all of the time, repeating this for every new INGO staff member that comes on board. 'No matter how involved we are, we can't keep every one of you informed all the time, we are not able to be available ad-hoc for everyone. We need time to do the primary work, that is assisting persons in need', they pleaded.

They also pointed to the scant resources raised. INGOs in Ukraine, for example, in addition to the mass amounts of funding received from the general public, received 6% of funds from the UN system too. Local CSOs, meanwhile, received a paltry share of 0.003% of the total. 'The facts speak for themselves: we don't have access to even a fraction of the funds that are at your disposal, and yet we do much of the work at the local level', they wrote.

All of the open letters – these multiple pleas for change – have several principles in common that signpost a new purpose and role for INGOs:

1. **They ask for equality and equity with international civil society.** They want their role to be made far more visible. This includes equality and equity in decision-making and in resourcing. This is stated very clearly in the openDemocracy letter of March 2020: '[o]ur plea is that you work with us not against us. We need to be supported, not competed with'.

2. **They ask for INGOs to play a more facilitating role** and to shed the role of gatekeeper. Instead, they want more direct relationships with funders, supporters, and policy-makers, not having INGOs speaking on their behalf.

3. **They see INGOs (and funders) as investors in their future.** Against the trend of 'localizing', like creating 'locally led' national offices, national and sub-national organizations would like to see INGOs as long-term investors in *their* work providing funds to help local civil society innovate, tell stories, and build their own long-term funding security. 'Invest in ways to help local people tell our own stories and to help us explain what we are doing to help. This supports deeper understanding and helps us to secure access to resources directly', we hear in the letter from Ukraine. 'Reduce your footprint and brand and use your fundraising machinery to help grassroots organizations create the structures to fundraise for themselves and sustain their work', states the openDemocracy letter.

These starter principles are a good jumping off point for redefining the role and purpose of INGOs and their place in the international civil society ecosystem. INGOs' historic purpose has evolved from one of solidarity to one of primarily delivering services or, in many cases, simply supporting the subcontracting role of governments. Instead, the new role should see INGOs facilitating, investing in, and enabling the role of national and local CSOs to take the spotlight, both in their own societies and internationally. This is especially important when national or local actors are directly implicated. The multiple principles from the open letter don't necessarily see an end to INGOs: rather, they see them filling an altogether different function and holding different relationships with national and sub-national actors.

Subsidiarity and the end of the North–South divide

Barbara Kingsolver, a Pulitzer Prize-winning American author, wrote her first novel situated in war-stricken 1960s Congo. *The Poisonwood Bible* focuses on a missionary family who go to 'save the unenlightened poor souls of Africa' only to be confronted by complex realities and a stark realization that their western knowledge is of little use here. Far from being superior, as they had assumed they were when they arrived, they lack either the practical skills or the political nous to survive, let alone help others. Kingsolver had lived in the Congo in the 1960s herself, her father a doctor wanting to indeed 'help the poor'. Her mission with the novel was to demonstrate the failure of American centrism, of neocolonialism offered in charitable form, and of the assumption that other ways of living and being were inferior to our own.

Decades later, in 2023, Kingsolver turned her attention in a new book, *Demon Copperhead*, to her home territory of Appalachia, a poor mountainous region of the US. Appalachia has many of the hallmarks of 1960s Congo, with poverty and exploitation at the heart of it. At least 20% of the population lives below the poverty line, and in one county alone, 20% have less than five years of formal education.[24] In this book, the main character is caught up in the opioid crisis, one which saw a multinational pharmaceutical company exploiting poor local populations.

We normally assume that Africa and the US bear little in common. But both the Democratic Republic of the Congo and Appalachia in the US have far more in common than one might assume when we think about the continents they inhabit. They have both suffered through the affliction of the 'resource curse', whereby mining companies extract wealth and leave little left to show for it. Both have high rates of poverty and deprivation. Both are, arguably, in need of 'development'.

Yet INGOs, by and large, still inhabit the world of Kingsolver's *The*

Poisonwood Bible, where missionaries with a white saviour complex find their way in Africa or Asia or Latin America to, ostensibly, 'save the poor'. They don't look at inequality or power at home. Much has been written recently about the white savour complex, including an excellent book edited by Themrise Khan et al.[25] But as the WACSI survey showed, a sense of western superiority continues to underlay relationships and the implementation of programmes by INGOs working abroad. Their unstated purpose remains to 'lead' or to 'teach' or 'to save' poor people of colour, generally living far, far away.

One of the great qualities of the UN's Sustainable Development Goals is that they rejected the framing that the North is wealthy and the South is poor. Instead, the signatories adopted universal goals for *all* countries, whether around social or environmental development. But surprisingly, this has yet to extend sufficiently into the evolution of global civil society, except in a few small circumstances.

There is a strong need for a global civil society to help bring together and connect our causes, wherever they happen to be. But we continue to be structured in a way that sees INGOs -- especially in development and humanitarian circles – as actors situated in the rich world who bring their skills and funding to poorer parts of the world. Human rights and environmental organizations have arguably been better actors in this regard, yet we still see few people living in richer parts of the world recognizing our own human rights or environmental spaces as something to save to the same degree as they do elsewhere. 'Oh, that wouldn't happen here', citizens of the UK tend to think. But think again we must.

Of course, all of the issues that INGOs work on are universal, be they human rights, poverty, equality, access to education, violence against women, or environmental matters. Thus, the specific role of the INGO – rather than focusing its work on 'elsewhere' – must be to connect national civil societies in common causes and support other civil society actors' ability to connect with people in their own contexts.

Political economists often refer to the concept of 'subsidiarity', which is a technical way of saying 'do what can be done locally, wherever possible'. This is as important for efficient administration as it is for building citizen action and engagement. How this applies to INGOs' role and purpose is central to the RINGO Project: how do we shift more power and resource locally, in the spaces that genuinely connect with people – the spaces where the hard day-to-day work is really done? And what does this mean for what we need from international civil society, aka INGOs?

There remains a strong and compelling case for practising both solidarity and subsidiarity. Arguably, we had an opportunity to put these concepts into practice when the war in Ukraine began in 2022, or when the COVID-19 pandemic took hold in 2020, which grounded INGOs almost instantly. Many were hopeful that these events would lead to a long-term shift in practices. Instead, in post-pandemic Ukraine, INGOs reverted to business as usual, sending 'missions' to assess needs and provide assistance, the anathema to solidarity and subsidiarity.

From saviour to solidarity

All of this speaks to the renewed role and purpose of the INGO. Many in the sector think we've gone beyond the saviour mentality, that relationships are stronger and deeper than ever before. But the realities suggest otherwise, and much of this is beyond the individual; it's caught up in the design of INGOs themselves. Though mindsets may be changing, the role and purpose needs to address two fundamental flaws in the current design of INGOs.

First, the purpose of INGOs must move away from 'helping the poor' or 'saving' anyone (including nature). Instead, the purpose should shift towards building solidarity; in so doing, the INGO can position itself not as leading the charge, but as in service to it. The INGO role then becomes one of facilitator, connector, enabler, or investor.

How could this work in practice? Imagine an alternative approach to how INGOs intervened in Ukraine. Instead of the usual situation, which saw INGOs needing to demonstrate their direct value-add through sending out people to 'assess needs', they could have invested the many millions directly in local CSOs. They could have invested in the development of an app, for example, to connect CSOs directly to European or North American or other richer world populations. They could have assumed the risk of international funding, without being gatekeepers, offering up core, unrestricted funding to local organizations – this is especially easy to do with the reams of unrestricted donations INGOs received from the general public. And they could have helped to convene safe spaces to let local CSOs decide and agree on what they wanted collectively – and in turn, sought to source it for them directly.

As became obvious from all of the work that RINGO did, and building on what many others have said: INGOs must move away from the saviour mentality. This isn't just a behavioural shift, but a shift in mindset too. They should embrace new roles as facilitators, connectors, and co-creators. For boards and leaders, these new roles will have significant implications on how INGOs function and their structure, which I explore in Chapter 3.

If INGOs were to revisit their mission statements to be both compelling and more apropos of this renewed role and purpose, they might now say: 'our purpose is to help create the connections and investment to enable civil society groups, wherever they may be, to work together and inspire people to build a just and good society'.

Marie-Rose Romain Murphy, a Haitian activist and community development expert sums it up well: '[i]f aid is really about ending the need for aid, shouldn't it be about Global South countries and communities getting to a point where they have a strong enough ecosystem that they don't need aid?'.[26] *This* should be the role and purpose of INGOs that we take as our starting point in the re-design.

CHAPTER THREE
From the inside looking out: Governance, structure, and skills

In September 2020, Amnesty International announced that it was closing down its operations in India. The government had frozen its bank accounts and accused it of circumventing foreign funding rules. The closure followed a series of ongoing and persistent attacks from the Hindu-nationalist Modi government on civil society. Narendra Modi, like many other populists, pursues an active policy of stifling dissent and democracy.

Modi's India and the rise of populism is central to the question of how we organize INGO governance and structure the organizations themselves. Since the early 2010s, Amnesty International pursued a vision of trying to move away from having all of their work led from London or the UK to creating a series of national offices, in order to build and grow the human rights movement around the world. For some years now, respect for human rights has been waning, as the western liberal-democratic 'consensus' that grew after the Second World War has come under increasing attack. Organizers in international civil society, alongside philanthropic endeavours, have rightly surmised that we need stronger civil societies everywhere to uphold and promote human rights and that the reliance on a network of international groups will never help if local people don't own the agenda.

Amnesty's intentions of setting up a separate structure in India – and other countries – was part of this aim, now known widely in technical terms as 'localizing'. Amnesty followed on the heels of others in the sector: in 2003, Action Aid created a federation of regional offices, headquartered in Johannesburg, and Oxfam International followed a few years later, setting up an international secretariat in Nairobi.

In 2012, when Amnesty came to India, there were already restrictions starting to impact on civil society's ability to function. The Foreign Contribution Relations Act, passed in 2010, created a huge barrier to organizations receiving any foreign funding into the country. Nonetheless, some local civil society leaders told me at the time that although it wasn't ideal, it would ultimately contribute to stronger local ownership of civil society.

But this hypothesis would prove to be misguided. Not long after Amnesty's arrival, in 2014, an Indian government Intelligence Bureau report accused foreign-funded NGOs, including Amnesty, of 'serving as tools for foreign policy interests of western governments' while harming economic development directly.[27] In this clearly egregious accusation, the report even went so far as to suggest that INGOs negatively impact on GDP growth by 2–3%. People working for Amnesty and other INGOs were attacked through spurious legal cases; some staff members were prevented from travelling abroad. It put an overwhelming chill on the entire civil society sector.

It no longer became viable for Amnesty or Greenpeace to function effectively in India. But the attacks didn't just harm the international sector: the Indian Home Ministry has blocked over 20,000 organizations from receiving foreign funds since 2012, forcing many others to close too.[28]

INGOs aren't to blame for the actions of a populist regime. But their entry raises some concerns. In other countries where Amnesty had localized, behind closed doors, national human rights actors accused it of using its brand name to poach funding and supporters away from long-standing local organizations, effectively cannibalizing the sector, rather than adding value. And whereas local organizations are able to seek change through means that give them influence and access, INGOs may rely on an approach that doesn't sit well in the local context. This raises the hackles of the government and, surprisingly, civil society too. As one senior person from an Indian environmental organization said to me shortly after the Intelligence Bureau report came out: 'Greenpeace ruined it for us'.

***

During the initial tide of populism's most recent ascent in the early to mid-2010s, INGOs were taken aback. They had been riding the wave of growing budgets, as aid targets were increased. The internet enabled faster, larger, and more targeted fundraising too. But in the face of attacks on their legitimacy by populist governments, INGO leadership took a reactionary approach. In several countries where causes were challenged by the government, be they human rights, environment, or development, the leadership of international civil society often unilaterally acquiesced in order to maintain access to that country: 'don't worry, we'll stop our work on human rights, and we look forward to staying here', they might have said. They gave the impression of 'neutrality' – that they were only there to support non-confrontational charitable objectives, helping the downtrodden poor. There have been many documented instances of INGOs halting any work that is publicly challenging power or converting human rights programmes to a focus on 'livelihoods' or 'humanitarianism'. On the face of it, it was a rational response to a complex problem. But this, in turn, has often left local organizations exposed or abandoned,[29] as INGOs prioritized access to countries over solidarity with local human rights organizers. Thus, governments were able to divide civil society and only keep those 'friendly' to them who wouldn't challenge their power. In the UK, a government minister urged NGOs to 'go back to their knitting'.[30] They wanted charity, not challenge. And, indeed, this attack on freedom of expression continues apace.

Arguably, the governance of many INGOs has sided with the 'knitting', fearing the wrath of regulators and the public gaze. Far from working in solidarity, organizations, driven by risk-averse boards, fundraising objectives, senior leadership, and even legal obligations, generally prioritize their own survival. In one workshop with INGOs I convened in 2018, discussing civic space, a senior fundraiser from a large INGO confidentially confessed, 'let's be honest, if another INGO gets kicked out of a country where we're working, we celebrate because that's more money for us'.

The vast majority of governance structures are designed to protect the institution itself, setting out goals, policies, procedures, and monitoring mechanisms for performance. As a board member, your job is to ensure the integrity and longevity of the organization. Legal, finance, human resources, and risk management are almost always at the top of the agenda for any INGO board, and boards themselves are charged with protecting the institution. So if there is a conflict or a risk of putting the organization in jeopardy, protection and risk aversion would naturally be prioritized. But if the mission of INGOs is to be geared towards supporting those they work with at the local level, then it would seem that the model of governance should change too. And this is a big step.

When Everjoice Win, an INGO leader, attended board meetings of her organization, she was overwhelmed with the disproportionate and almost all-consuming focus on risk management, rather than strategy or the mission of the organization: budgets, internal organizational policies and compliance, accounting, regulatory issues. It was all about protecting the organization. As she described to me:

> There was very little space for blue-sky thinking and really thinking about our role in social justice. We rarely discussed shifting power inside the organization itself. Whilst the role of the board should be organizational oversight, and not interfering in the day-to-day running of the organization, there also needs to be space to talk about its social justice, development role, and consistently reflect on how we are contributing (or not) to shifting power.

Protecting the organization seems to have become the de facto primary mission of governance, and, indeed, this is embedded into statutory obligations. Although you know that sitting on a board is an honour and a position of privilege – or perhaps a civic duty – there are times when you feel that this is penance for past behaviour, as you grind your way through the dry workings of management.

Yet, if we agree that the purpose and role of the new-model INGO is to build solidarity and strength of civil societies, then what the board is tasked with and who composes that board would seem to be the next point of departure.

There are examples of INGOs providing effective support to local civil society organizations (CSOs) in the face of attacks on civic space, including excellent campaigns like 'Protect the Protest' in the US, convened by Greenpeace.[31] But there remains a big question about the best structure and governance of INGOs. Can an INGO adopt a better governance model that more actively puts local civil society in the driver's seat and, if so, what would it look like?

Civic space, or 'the enabling environment for civil society' isn't the only driver that demands a rethink of standard INGO governance, but it is a strong one: if INGOs fail to function effectively at the national level, then they could cease operations altogether. Though there may be some positive reasons from a shift-the-power perspective for that to happen – and many local CSOs would agree with that – there are also some strong inherent risks. In the case of India, bringing down Amnesty brought a fallout for many other CSOs as well. This isn't to say that they wouldn't have come under attack anyway, but high profile organizations quite clearly exacerbated the situation, at least in the way they worked (or didn't) with local CSOs.

There are no one-size-fits-all approaches to structure and governance: but it's interesting to note that of the multiple models out there – be they federations of national organizations; top-down subsidiary models; membership models, etc. – all have, at one time or another, fallen foul of the power dynamics that arise relative to local organizations. Thus, no organizational model seems entirely immune.

What I've learned from over 25 years of working in civil society is that *process* is everything, and this is the heart of any governance model. And although structure and governance won't necessarily change everything, they can make a significant difference in helping to shift power. If you get the governance right, most actions an INGO takes to ensure more inclusivity will be on a stronger footing.

Legal accountability

Formal governance structures are there for a reason: they clarify who makes decisions and how to ensure accountability to funders, regulators, supporters, and members. There are some recent impressive attempts out there to be more directly accountable to communities, such as Save the Children's accountability audit.[32] But they all miss one key dimension: although they establish an intention to be accountable to those they are meant to serve, formal accountability to communities through any sort of legal means is entirely absent. It's a nod in a mission statement, an addition of 'voice' by adding a minority of board members from 'partner' organizations, or an annual advisory survey of key stakeholders.

The documents and policies are strong and growing in number, from safeguarding policies to stakeholder advisory boards, but the hierarchy of importance remains the same. By and large, all of the standard formal INGO governance models are built on upward accountability, upward management of risk, and upward decision-making. And while there may be broad statements, such as 'we are accountable to the communities we serve', practice doesn't necessarily equal the aspiration. The structure and governance of an organization is the starting point: like building a home, it can lay a stronger foundation for the new-model INGO going forward or it can be built on shifting sand.

Yolaina Vargas Pritchard, formerly of UK INGO network Bond, points out that current INGO governance is notably shaped by institutionalized racism and colonial mindsets, because there is a hierarchy of accountability.[33] You can see how accountability to trustees, funders, and government takes precedence over accountability to the communities INGOs serve. She writes:

> 'Typically, these structures and requirements can exacerbate power imbalances, evidenced in unequal pay structures, restrictive organizational culture (including fear of change), narrow definitions of "success" and whose voice counts'…. 'The communities that organizations serve are excluded from these processes and are often unable to hold an INGO to account'.

The starting point for governance is the legal statutes that set up international charities. In most countries where the vast majority of INGOs are registered or headquartered, they are generally accountable in law to 'their members'. Members are not, usually, the communities they serve: they may be individual supporters, boards of directors, or organizational members. Thus, there is already from the offset a huge gap in governance. INGO boards could be asking themselves: 'how can we formalize governance of our organization so that we are *genuinely and legally* accountable to the communities we serve?'.

There are models from the cooperative movement to draw from, which provide more inclusive ways to embed legal accountability to a wider net of stakeholders, but also as a way to hold each other to account.[34] Looking at what constitutes members and how their views are embedded in formal decision-making structures, including accountability, could revolutionize governance processes for many INGOs. 'The starting point is to democratize membership and think about representation of partner CSOs or the communities where you work', says Stephanie Biden, a partner at Bates Wells who advises UK-based charities, including INGOs, on their governance models. Biden acknowledges that very little has been done in INGO governance to move to a more locally led model. 'Amnesty, for example, has democratized the revenue side, in that individuals who join Amnesty as a funding member can participate in some level of its governance, but it's not a membership structure that reflects its local stakeholders', she says. And although including stakeholders more formally in governance is important, as Biden says, 'part of the challenge with any kind of membership structure is how you engage members so that their involvement in governance is meaningful and doesn't just feel symbolic'.

Newer business models?

Some organizations have shifted away from the limitations of charity or public benefit governance, adopting not-for-profit company models or social enterprise structures, for example. Though this can come with some constraints in terms of taxable benefits, it can also free organizations up from the limitations imposed on them as charitable organizations. These limitations can seriously restrict campaigning organizations, but they're increasingly impacting service delivery as well, imposing financial restrictions on receiving international philanthropic funding, for example.

In most jurisdictions, it's far easier to be more politically focused, to receive international funding or show solidarity with allies using a non-charitable structure. 'In a context in which regulatory environments and INGO organizational forms are another restriction on the INGOs really doing things differently, the private sector offers a genuine alternative', says Nicola Banks, a participant in the RINGO Project and founder of One World Together, a solidarity-based organization helping to provide long-term core funding support to allies. As a new start up working internationally with others, they registered in the UK as a community interest company (CIC) rather than a charitable organization, in order to be freed up from the constraints of the increasing number of restrictions on charities in the UK. The CIC model represents a non-profit business model that locks in assets to the cause, but has a far looser governance structure from the regulator. Instead of being overseen by a traditional board, it is collectively governed by its members and all profit stays within the community.

Governing for good: Return of the 5 'w's?

Those who grew up in English-speaking environments may recall our school teachers referring to the 5 'w's – who, what, when, where, and why – when teaching us how to construct a narrative. This lesson seems apt when we're looking at INGO governance of a new-model INGO.

Who?

Who makes decisions on whose behalf? INGOs aren't corporations making a product to sell. They are something different altogether. So why are the decision-making structures set up much like a company is?

Transform Trade (formerly known as Traidcraft) is a medium-sized INGO that originated in the UK. Transform Trade was a traditional organization, though it was firmly rooted in solidarity, having been borne out of the movement for trade justice. When the leadership wanted to decolonize, they adopted a strategy that puts funding allocation decisions in the hands of local communities, taking away their own power 'to decide'. This process has been incredibly brave, but also risky: at the time of writing, few funders wanted to get on board to help further this approach. Funders wanted more firm outcomes before offering up any money, and furthermore, didn't understand the shift from its traditional model.

Participation is central to a genuine effort to shift power and to how a new governance model might emerge from the ashes of a top-down neocolonial system. Fortunately, there are some models we can now look to for how this can work in practice. And the evidence is strong that participation will actually strengthen development.

Is it all white men making decisions at the top? Is a national office of an INGO localized if it continues to be governed by northern actors (as commonly happens). Should there be more diversity at the board level? Are there other structures that enable more diverse and multifaceted decision-making, like a cooperative structure? Could the idea of 'members' be extended to include communities?

What?

What are INGOs doing and what is the organization's purpose? It's not enough to bring in a more diverse board, because they could just as easily be indoctrinated into the old ways. Are they only looking at survival of the INGO? At accounts, risk management, or funding? How are they shaping the mission of the organization to accept more risk, or be more solidaristic and accountable to those they serve?

When a group of CSOs in a small and challenging country where civic space was rapidly closing approached RINGO to prototype an idea of a 'reverse call for proposals', they were doing so having been effectively abandoned by the international community, which felt that working in the country was too risky. They wanted help from INGOs and others but simply weren't getting it, and they were never even in a position to bid to be 'implementation partners' because there were no INGO projects on the ground at all. The idea behind the 'reverse call' was to get together as local civil society – human rights groups, women's organizations, development groups, and others – and make a plan for what they wanted and needed from the international sector, both financially and in-kind, in order to build their own more effective and stronger civil society. Unfortunately, they never got to the point of issuing a formal call for proposals before things took a backslide in the country and many of the actors were forced underground. But it was a strong challenge to the purpose of INGOs: is it to serve people on the ground? Or to serve the funding overlords? How can INGOs be *governed* to serve the former?

When?

Is the board only engaged in the few meetings a year or when there's a crisis? Are there more active forms of governance that breed wider ownership? When are decisions made – reactively or proactively? Social movements provide strong lessons in inclusive governance. Many have embedded deliberative processes in their day-to-day decision-making to ensure a constant engagement on the wider purpose and direction of travel. What can INGOs learn from social movements?

Where?

Is the INGO legally governed in London, Geneva, or Washington, DC, or has an organization 'localized'? Localization in this case, of course, isn't the panacea it seems to be. Imagine this: an INGO registers in a country in an effort to be more like a local organization. It then brings all of its resources to bear when promoting its brand locally. It seeks to attract membership from the local populations and bids on international grants that are intended for organizations from that country. The unintended result is that local INGO offices can displace local CSOs, cannibalizing from an existing local donor base.

A quick look at the structure of one organization, Médecins Sans Frontières (MSF), underpins this conundrum. Here, a complex web of operational partners, branch offices, and 'cells' see 'local' chapters as overt fundraising arms, and local associations as vehicles to promote the MSF brand identity.[35] It doesn't look dissimilar to a colonial governance structure from the 1800s or, perhaps more worrying, a complicated militaristic approach from the Second World War to ensuring all lines of defence are aligned.

Has the organization 'localized' in a way that gives it an unfair advantage over genuinely local organizations, giving it preferred access to donors and decision-makers? If the intention is to get closer to the ground, and to support a locally led INGO, is there an ethical way to do so that doesn't compete with local civil society? Do you really need to have a bricks and mortar presence in order to grow attention to your cause?

Danny Sriskandarajah, the former CEO of Oxfam GB, suggests that modern technology provides a way for there to be genuine distributed legal and organizational governance. Moving away from the bricks and mortar office and working remotely – wherever in the world teams may be – should also be matched with new and creative approaches to remote organisational relationships too. These new models should be explored in collaboration with local actors. Let us embrace this potential for all it's worth, though there are risks associated with technology that need to be explored (see Box 3.1).

Why?

Why is the organization even functioning locally? Is the role of the board just to protect the organization? In whose interest are they operating? INGOs do often have the advantage, with their brand, of being able to negotiate positions or make connections that local CSOs can't. But if they do this from a place of competition, rather than solidarity, they can easily undermine their cause. Can they focus on building and strengthening local civil societies' own assets? Is the deeper purpose hard-wired into the organization? Can they use their privilege to provide access where required?

There is unlikely to be a need for INGOs to provide direct delivery in the long term, except in circumstances where local civil society needs a buffer from complex politics. The role and need, however, should be agreed in collaboration with local CSOs. One way to do this is to formalize the process whereby local CSOs have regular and consistent input into the workplan or strategy of the organization, with this in turn fed into the local board and/or international board of the INGO. This is beyond the idea of a regular survey of stakeholders; instead it's a regularized and consistent consultation process that is built into organizational policies.

Structure: Do we have the skills?

Governance isn't all that we're talking about. The new structures that INGOs might adopt in future need to look at the skills they offer too. When Danny Sriskandarajah joined Oxfam GB in 2019, having come from an organization, CIVICUS, whose members were mainly from smaller organizations, he was astounded to find that Oxfam had 1,000 people working at its headquarters (HQ), occupying a large purpose-built building. The building itself was a symbol of the growth of INGOs in the late 1990s and early 2000s. With more income came the need to have more employees; with more employees came the need to have more income. The 2018 safeguarding crisis, which revealed shocking cases of sexual exploitation in the sector, provided the impetus to shift power, downsize, and create an organization more fit for purpose. But did it have the skills that were in demand or was it simply staffing to serve the needs of donors and to self-perpetuate their over-sized model? 'With size and brand, there comes a sort of centripetal force. You become ever more conscious of and protective of your brand, operating procedures, policies, and you need the people in place to do all of that. It is really important that the sector is conscious and avoids disempowering others', Sriskandarajah argues.

One can look at an organogram of most INGOs, regardless of the subject area of expertise, and it will look something like this: programme department, policy and campaigns, finance and human resources, and fundraising and communications. There will be variations within each of these, like 'conservation' for environmental organizations or 'logistics' for humanitarian organizations. There will be differing sub-headings within this, too, but the overall framework is pretty much standard. Job adverts for INGOs read more or less the same today as they did in the 1980s and 1990s: generic roles, like 'policy officer' or 'campaigner'; or specific skills sets, like 'gender equality' or 'monitoring and evaluation specialist'. These may, at times, be needed roles. But a new set of skills is needed for new-model INGOs.

A CEO at an INGO in the Philippines rightly complained to me about the fact that he was forced to write in a 'gender specialist' from the London-based HQ to a funding application. 'I have someone with a PhD in gender equality on my staff here in the Philippines – why do I need someone from London?', he asked. To him, it felt like a way to justify the HQ 'value-add' or, more cynically, to get more income for HQ, regardless of whether or not those skills were needed for the work at hand.

During the RINGO prototyping phase, several prototyping teams, working on different ideas to transform the sector, were looking for skills that didn't seem to exist in the sector or were so rare as to be impossible to secure. This was, in part, because they were in demand within organizations themselves, rather than in service to others: knowledge of artificial intelligence (AI), or block chain, for example, or next generation digital skills – useful in advocacy work, but equally important in distributed governance and funding models. AI is increasingly a topic that INGOs are looking at, but are the skills used in service to those they work with? Not yet.

Accountants who know how to reduce paperwork rather than adding another form are equally useful – that is, people who understand creative ways to manage risk and still meet legal requirements. Tick-boxers need not apply.

Adopting a 'reverse call for proposals' approach will certainly shine a light on the skills that are needed in INGOs to build solidarity models. If local CSOs would issue their own calls for partners to provide services or skills, this could transform the idea of funders or INGOs making decisions about what should be done and what skills are needed to succeed. Instead the real skills that are needed in INGOs should be locally defined based on local demand if organizations are genuinely working in service to local communities' needs.

Northern INGOs do probably still need policy expertise in order to lobby and influence their own governments. But these roles could probably be fewer than they currently are. More importantly, it can easily be argued that working collectively and sharing these roles across organizations, either through networks or coalitions, may be more effective and a better use of funding than having the same policy expertise duplicated across multiple organizations.

Questions for designing organizations should include: what roles are genuinely needed in an INGO? What roles can be shared through networks to ensure influence? How should organizations be structured to focus on solidarity and support a strengthened civil society overall, not necessarily a growing INGO?

In sum, new 'generic' skills in INGOs, commensurate with modern times, most certainly include things like AI, block chain, green economics, investment, online and offline facilitation, language and narrative, democracy and coalition building, and digital skills to underpin it. And they need to replace the old-style ones still predominantly in place. Mostly, we can say goodbye to northern 'experts' coming to save the poor. Local organizations have those skills already. The people-led, volunteer-based heart of INGOs may grow, whereas the 'professional class' should ultimately shrink.

A question of balance

'Can big be beautiful in civil society? Yes, if your brand power opens doors that otherwise wouldn't be opened, gets action or traction'. Sriskandarajah relays the story of attending meetings of heads of INGOs on the margins of large United Nations gatherings. He had been pleased to step aside during some of Oxfam's speaking slots to instead create opportunities for partner organizations to speak. But, he recalls, there were grumblings from some of his counterparts that they – mostly white, privileged male CEOs – weren't being given enough time to speak at these meetings themselves.

But big may not really need to be the big size that we know now. Oxfam GB, for one, is now down to almost half the size at HQ from what it was in 2018, with more resources going directly to partner organizations.

Tim Boyes-Watson, an expert in finance and governance of INGOs, has developed a theory of transformation of the INGO operating model. His looks at a range of INGO activities, from old style implementation and funder intermediaries to something altogether more modern: participatory grant-makers, facilitators, and advocates. And it's the latter of these that are lighter in nature: leaner organizations, not necessarily requiring offices, and with lower costs overall.[36]

The need for legal accountability to donors and 'members' will continue to be necessary, but, equally, what is needed are new forms of accountability – both formally and informally – to those the organizations are serving. And these multiple forms of accountability need not conflict. Doctors, for example, are accountable to both patients and professional governing bodies. Teachers are accountable to their employers (the state) and to parents and students. Every organization has multiple duties to fulfil – why not INGOs?

For INGOs, it's a question of having tipped the balance of power too much in one direction, primarily upwards towards donors. But the equation doesn't have to tip upwards in *favour* of funders and government. You can be accountable, and work in solidarity with those you partner with and the communities you're serving, while also meeting upwards demands. But the stated intent has to be matched with action in governance and the structure of an organization.

Box 3.1 AI: Disruption by stealth

There is a shocking lack of conversation in international civil society about AI, beyond some human rights organizations like Access Now. But a book about the future of INGOs, and wider civil society, is remiss if it ignores the role of AI. INGOs are not only going to face huge disruption from this sphere, if they haven't already; some say that it will 'revolutionise nearly every field of human activity'.[1a] It's creeping up on us ... and could swallow any sector plans before too long.

On the most basic level, AI automates the tasks of humans. Faster than we can imagine, it will easily supplant the role of INGO staff in the back office, automating everything from accounting and grant-reporting to logistics in the humanitarian space and even fundraising approaches. For smaller, local organizations, aspects of this can be positive: freeing up the inordinate amount of time spent on managing grants, for example.

As a tool, AI, or machine learning, is already far superior to humans in data analysis and in projecting trends. INGO policy wonks researching and analysing data around environmental or development trends could be all but redundant. AI will take on this role, and donors will probably expect it too; with the right systems in place, it can go further, deeper, and faster than any human analyst.

Areas of concern are obvious: civil society work will become more data-driven and could risk losing a human-centred focus; the ethics of data privacy and human rights are at risk, which is especially relevant in the context of building solidarity. INGOs like Access Now have been pivotal in building some civil society responses to these issues, which pose huge threats to every aspect of the world in which civil society engages. But these are only the tip of the iceberg; few INGOs outside of the human rights space are engaged at all in the major international policy conversations about AI. INGOs are still operating in a largely analogue world. But civil society, as the watchdogs and standard bearers, need to step up. What will the role of INGOs and other civil society actors be in addressing what Mustafa Suleyman, the co-founder of Google Deep Mind, refers to as 'the containment problem'?[1b] Even though the AI horse has bolted, we need to set some societal parameters on how it functions and how it can contribute to public good.

The digital divide, too, is a huge area of concern. The wealthier, larger organizations will be able to take advantage of the technology, whereas smaller CSOs will not, unless we are far more deliberate about engaging with both the threat and opportunity of AI in our efforts to shift power. For now, the sector lacks the skills to understand the technology and how to both defend its negative impacts on people and harness its advantages, ensuring fair and transparent distribution and application of its tools. We need to foster a stronger sense of AI literacy across civil society and this requires significant investment in both INGOs and national and local organizations. AI, like the corporate sector (see Chapter 5), is the elephant in the room for the future of INGOs, and needs to take a larger stage in the discussions around structure and governance of the sector.

CHAPTER FOUR
Managing risk and accountability

The Ombudsman Project, hosted by the British Red Cross in the 1990s, was one of the earlier attempts to hold INGOs accountable to those they serve. Its premise was that sometimes aid agencies do wrong, and they need feedback mechanisms to do better in future, alongside remedies for those who were failed.

The overall project said nothing about risk management to the organizations themselves: while donor-driven 'log frames', alongside other accountability tools, were commonplace, the idea of organizational risk management came more fully to the fore in the early 2000s. The critiques that inspired the Ombudsman Project didn't make it onto the front pages. They remained part of the internal machinations and introspection of the industry, as threats to the INGO brands weren't really on the radar, even as crises and scandals occasionally hit the headlines. Instead, the relatively enlightened view that local populations should be able to hold aid agencies to account for their actions was the primary frame. Advocates, like academic Hugo Slim and the Overseas Development Institute's John Borton, were paving an altogether more responsive and rights-based idea of humanitarian action in practice, as opposed to the heroic white saviour professionalized hero image that otherwise dominated the sector.

Sadly, like many efforts in humanitarianism over the past decades, the aims of the project ultimately got diluted from the desire to have an independent accountability mechanism – in this case an Ombudsman – to yet another form of self-regulation with very little accountability to local people in practice.

Ironically, as my first port of employment in the aid sector, the Ombudsman Project was where I learned how to fill out a log frame, that cumbersome table practice that forces you to draw a linear path between your work and a proposed outcome, as if social change can be entirely attributed to a single project, neatly and tidily, within a few years. This was despite the fact that the project was about accountability to 'beneficiaries of aid' (how we referred to them then). I also learned how to ensure upward accountability to appease the needs of donors and senior INGO leaders. Our actual practice was about anything but letting go of real power. It was a pivotal lesson for me in the contradictions hardwired into the system: we learned that INGOs will only let go of power with a donor incentive breathing down their necks – or worse, a public scandal. Moreover, INGOs are still so central to the system, that holding onto that power is paramount for their own survival. Donor practices of demanding theories of change actually enable INGOs to highlight their own perceived importance in change models, obfuscating the role of others.

Thus, the original moral argument for accountability to local people gradually became focused on the practice of risk management: implementing policies and procedures to avoid negative impacts, as opposed to those that hold organizations to account for their actions. The sexual exploitation scandals that befell the sector in 2018 were the pinnacle of this trend, resulting in the implementation of reams of paperwork, training, and procedures to ensure the safeguarding of local people. The burden of this was carried mostly by local CSOs or national branches of INGOs, with the assumption that local people can't be trusted and must be monitored.

Whereas accountability is the state of being liable and answerable, risk management is about avoiding or minimizing negative impacts. In and of itself, this isn't a problem. It's analogous, on paper, to the idea of prevention versus cure. In healthcare, this is applauded. But in practice, both risk management and accountability procedures are focused upwards, not downwards, in the system. This means that those at the top avoid as much risk as possible, relying on those at the bottom to bear the highest burden. This dominance drives the complex levels of risk management so prevalent in the system, and ultimately minimizes any accountability to local people.

This practice is one of the most fundamental systemic barriers to shifting power in the system. The imposition of bureaucracy by donors and INGOs in order to protect people and whole organizations along the value chain of civil society has come to supplant the idea of meaningful engagement. As a result, we don't have accountability as envisioned by the Ombudsman Project. Instead, we have transactional relationships based on mistrust and control.

Fortunately, in recognizing this to be the case, it's an issue we can do something about.

Current practices of risk management and accountability

In 2023, international peacebuilding initiative Conducive Space for Peace published a study summarizing the current practice of risk management, which originates from funders, highlighting how it actually inhibits local actors' abilities to deliver and grow their own organizations. They analysed how a complex 'chain of influence' creates a hierarchy of interest, whereby public and private donors and the United Nations (UN) system passes risk down the chain: to INGOs and ultimately to local organizations.

Here's how it works: a government mandates a certain amount of spending in the aid budget; that funding goes to the aid agency, which is required to spend it through various means: UN agencies, INGOs, or the private sector. Funds may only then reach national or local organizations. But at every level, an accountability procedure – usually associated with a financial cost – is added in: for administrators, finance officers, international advisers, programme managers, fundraisers, and monitoring and evaluation staff.[37] Procedural burdens to manage risk are added both externally – on actors who eventually get access to some funding – and internally, with risk and compliance procedures to protect everyone along the chain.

From the perspective of a national or local CSO, staff may be required to fill out dozens of forms to prove that they have mechanisms in place to prevent misuse of funds; that they've undertaken safeguarding or financial management training; that they have policies in place; that they have auditors to check that they have policies in place and viable accounting procedures; that they have whistleblowing provision; that they have managed complex projects in the past; that none of their staff or board members have ever been involved in mismanagement in another organization; and that they have a sufficient number of peers who can vouch for them. For local civil society organizations (CSOs), in particular, this is as far away from their actual work of engaging with local people as they can possibly get.

In one study that RINGO undertook in the Philippines, as part of a prototype project on risk, there were 52 requirements from the US Agency for International Development (USAID) that the Centre for Disaster Preparedness, a Philippine CSO, was assessed for in order to access any funding. This included everything from governance and control (such as fraud, bribery, risk management, and ethics), ability to deliver (capacity, management, and past performance), financial stability (management, auditing, and value-for-money), and relationships with other partners. In Ukraine, amidst an ongoing conflict, local CSOs waited up to six months after filling out multiple forms in order to secure funding in some cases.[38]

No wonder local CSOs suffer a huge disadvantage: they have a smaller number of staff, limited fundraising and admin capacity, often no core funding, and they're trying to get work done on the scraps of what is left to them from the top of the value chain at the same time as proving they have systems in place worthy of a multi-million-dollar, multi-national corporation. Effectively, you have to be an affiliate of one of the large global accountancy firms, like PwC, regulated by the US Securities and Exchange Commission, in order to receive a small grant from an INGO or donor.

Understanding the drivers

Risk aversion among public donors is high for some very good reasons. Politics has long been a factor in challenging aid budgets in the first place, as in: 'why should our government be spending money in some "shit-hole" country [to steal a phrase from Donald Trump] instead of at home?' a typical right-wing rant might read. A civil servant working in USAID once admitted to me: 'we don't care if a US INGO wastes a million [dollars], but we care if a small CSO in Nigeria wastes one [dollar]'. He didn't agree with the sentiment, but it was something he had to constantly confront in his day-to-day working environment. It was the realpolitik of the aid business.

In the UK, it's the *Daily Mail* tabloid that politicians and civil servants often try to appease. In 2014, the newspaper ran a front-page petition calling on the government to divert the aid budget to be spent locally on a flooding emergency at home, pitting poor people abroad versus the UK population. In 2022, it was behind a campaign to temporarily cut the foreign aid budget amidst an economic downturn, and it has called out the government for spending money in countries that won't get behind the UK on Russia.[39] The right-wing tabloid press has been fairly successful at breaking down a long history of public support for aid overseas. Regardless of the assumption about neutrality, politics matter to INGOs, even if only in terms of how they are portrayed by conservative forces.

Since 9/11, the practice of risk management has grown exponentially, as INGOs and those who are in receipt of their funds were in the crossfire of the clampdown on terrorism, and the commensurate upswell of waves and waves of anti-terrorism measures imposed by all western countries. The Funders Initiative for Civil Society has documented the rise of counterterrorism laws that have resulted in labelling many CSOs as terrorists or terrorist sympathizers, especially those who focus on supporting Muslim communities, like Islamic Relief. Many saw their bank accounts closed down and, if not, huge increases in bureaucracy in order to move funding around the globe.

The consequence of 9/11 Is now the myriad of laws, not only aimed at trying to reduce the ability to shift money between countries, but also aimed at stemming activism – and managing so-called risk. It's a wide net: it has impacted every organization involved in human rights, animal rights, development, and more. So an organization in a non-western country might get a red flag tagged on them if a government wants to use this in a way to control their work. They are all guilty until proven innocent.[40] Thus many CSOs outside western countries have had ongoing challenges trying to access financial services; without banking provision, organizations can't accept funding. The layers upon layers of bureaucracy are often disincentives for local CSOs to partner with INGOs or others, even on an unequal basis.

Some of the laws that are baked into the system end up prioritizing INGOs in practice: the practice of 'tied aid', discussed in Chapter 5, prioritizes a country's own INGOs for domestic funding. In Canada, for example, tax laws have required funding aimed at local organizations to go through an INGO by default. The assumption being that the INGO can better manage any risk associated with charitable activities, like corruption.[41]

In these ways risk management has overpowered accountability to those served. Ideally, in the long term, effort should be placed on both of these areas. First, effort is needed to tackle inequality at home, which enables conservative politicians to divide causes. Then, INGOs can build a greater sense of solidarity with people in other countries again, through narratives and the media. And finally, they should advocate for a shift in counterterrorism laws. These are all worthwhile endeavours that some organizations are working on already. In the short-term, more practical approaches can help to kick-start a transformation in the right direction.

Perceptions matter

There is no more risk in funding local CSOs than there is in funding INGOs. Indeed, the perception that it is more efficient or less risky to fund an INGO may be a myth. The real risks of fraud or corruption are also hugely overstated: the UK's Independent Commission for Aid Impact found that less than £0.01 per every £100 of aid money spent is ultimately lost to fraud.[42] They nonetheless recommend policies of further checks and balances, because, as they state 'every penny counts'.

Racism and mistrust play a strong role in driving current practice too. This was encapsulated by a conversation I had in the early days of the RINGO Project with a former CEO of one of the world's largest INGOs. An elder white American man, he said very bluntly: 'why would you want to give more money and power to local organizations? They're all corrupt'. Perceptions matter. We come back to structural racism when we look at funding, but it's worth stating now that structural or institutional racism is so embedded in our institutions and is perhaps *the* primary driver for upwards, ever more bureaucratic, accountability procedures.

Although donor organizations are often the first initiator of heavy-handed accountability procedures, INGOs themselves have also played a significant role in imposing more bureaucracy and checks on organizations, often imposing their own sets of checks and balances on those they partner with. A simple call for expressions of interest for potential partners by Christian Aid in Nigeria asked for evidence of everything from how they handle cash and where it is kept, to the qualifications of the auditors, alongside a full description of their participatory monitoring, evaluation and reporting system.[43] Any sense of trust building and solidarity seems to have disappeared in the mountain of bureaucratic paperwork.

US INGO Network Interaction found that in humanitarian work, risk management comes up against some countervailing forces: legal constraints, imposed from donors; intensifying financial scrutiny, either by donors or the general public; and the repercussions of things going awry and hitting the front pages in highly volatile and high-risk environments. All of this goes against the demand for less bureaucracy and more trust. Systems were imposed on those organizations working on the front lines because of the perception that they were risky – not that they, themselves, faced huge risks.[44]

The sexual exploitation scandals that emerged in 2018, which exposed severe breaches in safeguarding by a number of INGOs added on further layers of bureaucracy and upwards accountability to every UN agency and INGO the world over, who passed these onto their partner CSOs, contractors, and everyone in between. I had a seven-day research-based consultancy contract for a UN agency in 2020 which required me to undertake over a day's worth of safeguarding and sexual harassment training, even though the work was desk-based and had no involvement with local people whatsoever. It is absolutely critical to protect against sexual exploitation, but imposing such systems isn't about the victims or even the culture of the organization: it's about protecting an organization and enabling them to say 'we've done our job'.

During the course of the RINGO Project we also heard about systems being imposed on local organizations, not at the requirement of donors, but by INGOs' own internal systems of control, which were set up to protect the INGO brand. It wasn't just an academic exercise and, to some extent, it was understandable. The damage to organizations like Oxfam or Save the Children in the wake of the 2018 scandals led to the full suspension of donor funds, alongside significant loss in membership from individual supporters. Several INGO leaders have anecdotally said to me that it took five years before their membership and income levels began to recover.

Be reasonable

The reality is that there *is* risk associated with any sort of funding, whether it's in the US, the UK, or Europe – or indeed in aid funding to recipient countries. But that risk isn't confined to civil society; it could happen in government sectors, where the bulk of aid is delivered directly, or in the corporate sector, where a significant amount of aid increasingly goes.

Nonetheless, although risk may need to be managed, proportionality is in order here. The levels of bureaucracy imposed on local civil society is simply not commensurate with the actual risk at play, nor does it recognize that local actors are the ones facing most of the risk, not INGOs or donors.

Local CSOs are on the front lines of the risk equation: they take risks to work with donors and INGOs, especially where civic space is narrowed or closed. They hold the burden of safety risks, security risks, legal compliance, reputational risks, ethical risks, and data risks. The list goes on.

The obvious and most oft-cited solution to reducing the risk burden is to allow more core funding to go to organizations, rather than only to specific projects. This would immediately reduce paperwork and undue controls over relatively small sums of money, freeing up time and capacity of national or local CSOs and reducing the need for INGOs, working as intermediaries, administering their own sets of checks and balances. It's a call that's been reiterated for decades now, but is still rarely taken up by donors, either government or philanthropic. Why not? Circle back to our discussion earlier: racism and trust are the underlying reasons, rather than actual risk.

A more radical approach is to look at risk management in a wholly different way: as something that needs to be co-agreed and negotiated. Recognizing that risk needs to be managed and that some upward accountability is needed to satisfy donor governments, negotiated risk would bring all parties together to ask: how do we share this risk, who should face the burden, and how do we satisfy the needs of all constituents here?

Plenty has been written on risk. There are multiple case studies of 'good practice' and an infinite number of case studies of 'bad practice'. There is a frequent mantra about not passing on risk, but instead looking at risks to the organizations on the ground and sharing it – judging by how frequently its discussed, one would think that the practice would be as common as brushing your teeth. Yet time and time again, the reality bears little resemblance to the rhetoric.

The RINGO risk and compliance prototype sought to innovate risk management by transforming it from a bureaucratic approach to something altogether more revolutionary. Instead of imposing a complex compliance system, the RINGO prototype convened a 'brave encounter' between the hidden actors in the system – in donor organizations, INGOs, and local CSOs. In INGOs, these are often staff members who are less visible, but more likely to impose controls and bureaucratic burdens on recipient organizations. This includes the finance officers, compliance officers, and programme officers, among others. The aim of the prototype was to see if risk could be negotiated and if what is reasonable and proportionate (see Box 4.1) and what is not in a particular case could be agreed. I know from experience that you may be offered a grant from a programme officer (in either a government or philanthropic organization) only to have to go through a whole series of hurdles once the administrative side comes into play. A manager gives a 'yes', which seems like a celebration, then the complications follow. This increases exponentially if you're a CSO in a non-western country.

***

The findings of the first 'brave encounter' – involving USAID, Global Giving, and the Philippines based Centre for Disaster Preparedness (CDP) – were revealing. The meeting participants agreed that donors are risk averse because of their accountability to taxpayers and that this is the reason for the long provisions in grant agreements, alongside the US laws and regulations that underpin these. This minimizes their flexibility. Systems, however, are inflexible: USAID, for example, runs potential grantees through an international terrorist list compiled by the national government (in this case, the Filipino government). If civic space is closing, governments will 'red flag' an organization as terrorists if they run counter to the government of the day.

The conversation itself was a starting point to understand what's driving undue risk management systems from all sides, and began to identify what may be more reasonable in practice: in this case, rather than the system of checks through the international terrorist list, the participants proposed that a peer-to-peer certification system to assess the character of an organization could be a better model for due diligence and risk management. They are now looking at investing in a locally led system that can do this.

Box 4.1 What do we mean by 'proportionality'?

Is it reasonable to have to collect a receipt for every piece of paper bought for a project? No. But this is common practice. Aside from the bureaucracy, this can be of much greater risk to the grant recipient or partner, especially in countries where human rights are at risk, as it provides a paper trail from activists who would prefer to meet safely and confidentially.

Is it reasonable to have to get quotes from three stationery providers before purchasing a ream of paper? No. But this very thing is often required and I have heard of one case where an organization lost funding because they allegedly paid too much for stationery.

Is it reasonable to expect an entire organization to be audited separately to their usual process? No, it absolutely is not. But large funders often insist on this if a grant exceeds a certain amount, say US$50,000 or even $20,000. This presents a huge barrier to growth for organizations in Africa, Asia, and Latin America, duplicating work and increasing costs.

Other areas of concern were assumptions about capacity: most risk management and due diligence systems – indeed, the 52 indicators – were about these assumptions of what counts as 'capacity', which are almost always western-defined. 'Unfortunately, the assessment of who has "capacity" has been weaponized and used as a means to justify the slow relinquishment of power by INGOs and their hollow promises of localization. We require more individuals actively engaged in community work and fewer confined to their desks, endlessly reporting to donors', writes Michael Vincent Mercado of the CDP.[45]

The CDP recently took on an opportunity to support more local grant-making. As an organization, they were used to receiving funds from large donors, like USAID. They would normally be required to provide details about 52 areas of risk management in order to receive the funds. Inspired by the work of the brave conversation, they were able to negotiate a reduction in risk checks from 52 to 1 for sub-grants to local organizations that were roughly equivalent to US$22,000.

Though the 'brave conversation' idea needs more testing in practice, it paves a way for a new way of thinking about risk and managing it collaboratively. It acknowledges that while there may be risks in a funding or partnership relationship, building trust is far more important. It challenges us to address what might be proportionate, and, most importantly, how best to share the risk burden across all stakeholders. A start of any relationship between INGO, donor, and local CSO could begin here.

Who should be accountable to whom?

The 1990s Ombudsman Project was a laudable example of trying to turn accountability systems on their head by suggesting that INGOs, and the wider aid system, are the ones to be held to account by local people. But it never saw the full light of day as originally envisaged.

Marie-Rose Romain Murphy, a community development practitioner, writes: '[t]he reality of the aid construct is that it is structured and animated towards sustaining itself with an accountability system catering to donors ... there are no set institutional metrics for an accountability process to communities. It isn't even a thought'.[46]

Sadaf Shallwani and Shama Dossa argue that accountability is reinforced by 'white saviourism' through the imposition of mainstream evaluation processes. They find that western-educated, predominantly white people are perceived to be better placed to decide and do on behalf of local people, in the interests of delivering 'charity'. 'Evaluation in global development centres on the White subject as doer, the Saviour and the neutral expert ... [who] identifies deficits and problems in the lives of Black and Brown people and demonstrates how interventions designed and funded by the Global North are necessary and effective – thereby reinforcing the feel-good element of the White Saviour'.[47] Though there may be evaluators of colour, they are trained to internalize these views, assumptions, and practices.

Local people may have some participation in evaluation processes, but it is ultimately the assessment of a northern-based (usually) white person from the outside who determines a project's success. Those on the ground are not, in any way, holding international actors to account. As a participant at a webinar about decolonizing aid stated, 'From my experience of evaluation for the past 14 years, I have come to conclude that, whoever pays the evaluator, whoever develops the Evaluation Indicators dictates the outcome of an evaluation'.[48]

Bottom-up accountability

The Pledge for Change is a radical attempt to genuinely decolonize INGOs. It's led by Adeso, an East African humanitarian organization whose CEO, Degan Ali, has been at the forefront of the movement to shift power to local CSOs. Fed up with all words coming from the sector and no action to accompany it, she convened her own initiative with the CEOs of some of the largest INGOs in the world. Together, they have 'pledged' to make headway in key areas of change, from shifting funding and power to using their influence to ensure stronger local and national civil societies.

The Pledge participants also wanted to use this as an opportunity to demonstrate how local actors can hold INGOs to account, in a bottom-up and altogether different way than conventional methods, where accountability is driven by the power holders in INGOs or donors, and ultimately is more about managing risk. With conventional approaches, the emphasis is on reporting upwards through metrics, studies, and reports. The Pledge looked to more collective forms of accountability – non-technocratic, peer-to-peer, and community based – that are already widespread in local civil societies in Africa and elsewhere and that place local people as the evaluators of INGO practice.

Trust and mutuality are at the heart of this. Isabella Jean, the coordinator of the work, says 'much of accountability and feedback often becomes technocratic … but at the community level, if we think about the best community organizing approaches, they are relational. Community organizers build relationships and trust, and mobilize – they don't show up with indicator surveys'.[49]

Accountability should be about transparency and learning – not punishment. But there are challenges. It's much easier to go around with a checklist and ask 'do you have this system?', 'do you have that system?', or 'how many people were fed and watered?' than it is to convene a dialogue of all the actors and ask 'what does success look like for you?', 'what have we learned?', 'what did we do wrong?', and 'what could we do better?' in a trusting and open way. Social change is messy and these new models of accountability acknowledge that.

Risk, accountability, reward

For INGOs, this demands new skill sets and investment in time, with commensurate resources. It also demands vulnerability and the space in which to make mistakes – and be able to admit to them. This doesn't fit with current evaluation practice. Funders don't like this, and INGOs find it hard to report on this. INGOs need to consider how they should be accountable to communities, not the other way around, in the way that I, as a citizen, expect my own government to be accountable to me. This means practising radical transparency and turning the whole notion of risk and accountability on its head.

For funders, the need to let go is even more paramount; asking who is really taking risks, and how can they be held accountable to those taking the risks, would be a good starting point. Changing mindsets will ultimately change systems. For private philanthropy, this is a massive change of direction, and requires systemic change through every level of an organization: from the compliance officer to the board.

As with all of our areas of work around a re-imagined INGO, the heart of this work is about trust and building a stronger ecosystem for civil society. 'The charity sector should be valued for how it reduces risks to society and judged by how effectively overall it does this', says Ed Mayo, the CEO of Pilotlight.

It's the very foundations that will enable us to tackle all of the more difficult issues we're facing externally. Divided civil societies are enabled by the systems of mistrust as engineered by our current risk and accountability systems: they are the opposite of creating a nurturing environment in which civil society can genuinely thrive in order to pursue the real business of improving their societies.

Instead, place the emphasis on relationship building, not necessarily outcomes. Let communities decide what success looks like. Reduce the bureaucracy. Create something proportionate jointly with others. Make the indicator of success a stronger civil society in and of itself.

CHAPTER FIVE
Show me the money

When Degan Ali, the Director of Adeso, stood up at meetings leading up to the 2016 World Humanitarian Summit's now landmark Grand Bargain commitment to see 25% of funding going to local civil society organizations (CSOs), she accused the aid sector of racism and neocolonialism. It sparked an outcry. Ali had been leading her African non-governmental organization for some years and was fed up with the crumbs of funding that were coming her way. Despite having a budget of over US$13 million at the time, and Adeso being one of the only organizations working on the ground in Somalia, none of the funding was unrestricted – meaning Ali had no flexible funding to support staff or build the organization. Behind closed doors, people told her to keep quiet and to stop pissing off 'those people in power'.

At various points in Ali's career, she was often marginalized and tokenized, generally wheeled out to impress funders about their inclusiveness but not there to actually contribute. She relayed a memorable incident where an INGO 'partner', represented by a white man, asked for her ideas about what to do in Somalia, her own country. Whereas the INGO wanted some funding for a basic water rehabilitation project, she thought cash transfers would be more successful, and far more likely to help the local population. But she was told by the man not to share the idea and that she didn't know what she was talking about. 'I was the only black person in the room, the only person from Somalia. I was there as a showpiece', she told me. Towards the end of the meeting, she ignored the advice and relayed her thoughts about why cash transfers were so important in a context like Somalia's pastoralist society. As would be the pattern for Ali, ignoring the advice of INGOs and, in particular, white men in power, has paid off. The donor accepted the idea and it became one of the pioneering large-scale cash transfer projects in the country.

Thankfully, Ali had the tenacity and perseverance to lead the charge up to the 2016 World Humanitarian Summit too. She spent two gruelling years fighting for a minimum target that would bring more resources to the organizations on the ground who were doing the lion's share of the work, and, importantly, for representation. 'Global South actors were excluded from key groups like the Grand Bargain Sherpa group, the negotiating body for the Grand Bargain', she says, 'so we had to rely on allies on the inside'. She faced attacks from all sides: from the INGOs, donors, and United Nations agencies who thought she should stay in her place, and even from local humanitarian organizations who rightly felt that they should have a larger share of funding than her original target of 20%. 'We do 80% of the work', they urged her, 'so why only 20%?'. But she wanted something to aim for that was achievable, and, at the time, a meagre 1.2% was reaching local actors.

Ultimately, the summit committed to an ambitious target of 25% of aid reaching local organizations by 2020, ushering in what many hoped would be the sunset years of western-led and delivered humanitarian aid. This was in recognition of the fact that local civil societies were more than capable of tending to their own needs, even in times of humanitarian crises – if only they had the means to do so.

Sadly, by 2024, that commitment – and others that came before and since – has been nowhere close to being reached. Ali has continued to persevere, both with trying to persuade the wider sector to mend its ways, through, among other things, her initiative called 'the Pledge', but also through setting up her own investment vehicles to reduce the reliance on northern-based philanthropy and aid expenditure, aided in part by a commitment from philanthropy.

Accessible funding remains the cornerstone for successful civil society everywhere. And while most bilateral donor governments have still not met a long-held target of spending 0.7% of gross domestic product on aid, what is available for civil society is spent mainly through the international sector, with an estimate of 93% of funding aimed at civil society going to northern-led INGOs.[50] Though data is patchy, it's fair to assume a similar picture for philanthropy. In fact, some research shows that things are actually getting worse for local CSOs. Though the absolute amount of funding has grown, the share that they receive has, in fact, declined since 2015,[51] in spite of efforts like the recent donor pledge to increase local funding led by USAID and underpinned by philanthropy.[52]

Why is it so difficult to get funding to local civil society despite the general consensus that more needs to be done? The reasons for this are rooted in a combination of structural racism and politics, all reinforced by legal and technical barriers[53] that many think are just too much to overcome.

Structural racism

In the early days of the COVID-19 pandemic, the Black Lives Matter movement rose to prominence on the international stage. Though the movement had been around for some years, it was amplified when George Floyd, an innocent black man, was murdered by white police officers in Minneapolis, US. It was an increasingly common occurrence, but this time it was captured on video for all the world to see. Enough was enough. Protests rose up in cities across North America and Europe and sparked a wider introspection about racism in every sector, not just civil society.

The moment was, and remains, a strong reckoning for the INGO and philanthropic sectors. The movement gave rise to a voice that had, for years, been suppressed in the sector, finally enabling people to more openly call out the institutional racism that was hardwired into the system. Dylan Mathews from Peace Direct, an organization that has since led many INGO-wide discussions on anti-racism, explains:

> We looked at this in a lot of detail after George Floyd. I had a strong sense that this was one of the missing pieces of the puzzle about why the sector hadn't moved forward. We asked our partners 'do you see this as a problem?' and they said firmly, 'of course it is, please talk about it, because we won't talk about it'. They had never mentioned it before and were self-censoring, because they didn't want to be seen as troublemakers and didn't want to be vilified.

The UK-based organization Charity So White emerged around the same time. They define racism as 'the power and the elevation of some populations to positions of primacy and domination and the denigration and subordination of others'. They describe institutional racism as racism 'enacted and reproduced in the main by institutional forces in society'.[54] Another definition of structural racism refers simply to ways of 'feeling, being, and doing that are deeply woven into the fabric of an organization and that advantage white people and disadvantages Black and Indigenous people and people of colour'.[55]

Institutional or structural racism plays out at the organizational level in funding and civil society in multiple ways: it affects who gets access to funding and who makes decisions, and it puts barriers in place to prevent local civil society groups from accessing funding, due to bias and lack of trust. It manifests itself in the implementation of funding, through detailed budgeting procedures and auditing processes. Research consistently shows that white people and 'white ways of doing things' (aka western) are considered more professional, more expert, more reliable, and more valid.[56]

'The problem with structural racism is that it's so insidious. It's under the radar – it's structural as opposed to always overt', says Shaheen Kassim-Lakha from the Hilton Foundation. 'Especially within a global context, it's so layered. It's about who has access to those who have access to those who have access', she says.

The response to this in the sector has been slow, with diversity, equity, and inclusion efforts aiming to recruit more people of colour to boards and senior leadership as the predominant response. But even changing positions on boards or in staff bodies, although important, isn't the only answer. People of colour may be afraid to 'rock the boat' and may adopt the institutional way of doing things, with English-language speaking and western-educated people still dominating in international spaces. 'As someone coming from Africa in the context of being an immigrant in the US, I had to really play down the concerns around structural racism, because that's not a winning point for a first job', observes Kassim-Lakha.

Added to the complexity is the imposition of rules and regulations that start from a position of mistrust, as touched on in the previous chapter. These rules are rooted in structural racism and a white bias: we trust INGOs to be accountable; we don't trust people of colour.

Structural racism is one of the main drivers that keeps INGOs in a place of power in civil society, because it's a well-known truism that those in positions of power, mainly white people, are unwilling to give it up, and that it's hardwired into our system.

'The international development profession has consciously and unconsciously impeded progress in the Global South, not accelerated it ...There needs to be a tectonic shift in how white saviours have been conditioned by decades of colonialism to consider racialised people inferior', writes Themrise Khan et al. in their edited book on white saviourism.[57]

This is where the funding comes in. Is there something that funding flows, and those who are in charge of them, can do to help incentivize a new model? And are there new models of funding that remove some of the power of the donors and INGOs – and places them in the hands of local people? As a lever for change, money is a pretty powerful driver, and the RINGO Project, alongside others, has been exploring how best to use the funding lever as a way to shift power.

It starts at the top: Official development assistance

Official development assistance (ODA) can make up a very large share of civil society funding. At least US$24 billion per year go directly from ODA to CSOs,[58] including both large and small CSOs. For many years now, there has been a drive to ensure that a larger share of the funding goes to local organizations, at least on paper.

The World Humanitarian Summit was just one of many long-standing commitments by governments to increase funding to local CSOs. In fact, even this bold commitment was not exactly new. As far back as 2001, Organisation for Economic Co-operation and Development (OECD) governments had made commitments to ensure more funding goes to local organizations, by abolishing the practice of 'tied aid' – the practice that sees aid funding going directly to OECD countries' own civil societies as intermediaries. They acknowledge that the practice is costly – adding up to 30% of direct costs – and goes against efforts to build stronger civil societies in the face of closing civic space.[59]

In 2021, USAID made a commitment to increase local civil society funding to 25% of its overall budget by 2025, with an aim to reach 50% by 2030. When the policy was announced, Samantha Power, USAID Administrator, said, '[i]f we truly want to make aid inclusive, local voices need to be at the centre of everything we do'.[60] As the largest government donor in the world, what USAID says and does matters a great deal. Although it acknowledges the importance of

INGOs as intermediaries, as part of this policy, USAID also wants INGOs to shift away from leading and doing and has committed to start measuring efforts towards this goal.

Could this act alone spell the end of INGOs? Unlikely. As with any commitment, the devil is often in the detail. It is estimated that of the 7% of bilateral funds that reach local CSOs directly, only 1% goes to core support. The remainder is restricted and allocated to donor-initiated projects. Funding can be directed to local organizations, but if it remains aligned to those projects that aren't designed and led by local actors – with multiple restrictions – the original intent will ultimately be undermined.

In most (if not all) OECD countries, there are significant legal barriers still in place that serve to counteract any laudable commitments, like USAID's. In Sweden, for example, one of the key limitations of the government approach is its insistence on diverting funds through INGOs. Sweden has a zero-tolerance policy on corruption, and demands a complete repayment on any supposed misspent funds. This breeds fear and inertia: it's easier to stay the course, with the assurance of INGOs, than it is to take risks. 'In Sweden and in many other countries, we are very serious about corruption. We have zero tolerance about corruption. And we assume that the Swedish INGOs are not corrupt, yet we seem to assume that Global South local CSOs are, and therefore they need to be closely controlled and monitored', says Viveka Carlestam, of the Swedish International Development Cooperation Agency.

Meanwhile, INGOs wield significant power, ensuring that their voice and access to funds remain centre stage. Aside from the armies of finance officers and the resources to track funding in order to reassure donors, they have regular and direct access to donors and politicians, too, to cement their place in the funding hierarchy. INGOs use this access to persuade them of their 'value-add' and the need to keep funding dominance in place.

Even when I was leading a fairly small campaigning organization in the UK, we had quarterly dinners in the House of Lords with other INGO leaders, with government ministers often invited to the table. This was the regular, informal access to decision-makers. More formal meeting requests with ministers or senior civil servants were always granted. This privileged access maintains INGOs' positions – and the funding that follows. Until 2024, Sweden provided their national INGOs with a renewable five-year grant, to which 1.9 billion SEK per year (approximately US$175 million) was channelled.[61] And although other countries, like the UK, have also stopped their guaranteed multi-year grants to their domestic sector, not all have. Other countries give priority to their own INGOs, Germany and Canada among them. The reasons may be subtle (say, taxation) or they may be overt (say, anti-terrorism).

There is an assumption underpinning these relationships – it is assumed that this is simply a more efficient way of giving. Surely it's easier to give to 1 INGO than to 20 smaller organizations? Not so, says the actual research. Giving through INGOs actually costs more, as the OECD has finally acknowledged. Research from Shared Interest shows that 'local intermediaries can deliver programming that is 32% more cost efficient than international intermediaries, by stripping out inflated international overhead and salary costs'. It estimates that, '[a]pplied to the ODA funding flows allocated to UN/INGOs in 2018 ($54bn), this would equate to US$4.3bn annually'. The researchers modelled the data using more equitable rates rather than business-as-usual rates. They argue that inflated rates charged by INGOs actually 'impede local actors from meeting the needs of their communities, resulting in an additional redeployment of $680m per year in salary and overhead costs to local actors'.[62]

Arguably governments like these allegiances, not just for their (mis)perceived convenience and efficiency, but also because it helps them exert their soft power: INGOs can be an instrument of soft policy and influence. Thus, INGOs and governments, through their funding, have a symbiotic relationship.

The key long-term action to changing this is to address the structural racism inherent within this relationship, and the views around mistrust. This requires better narratives and storytelling, to situate local CSOs in the best light, not the worst. INGOs can help with this, both through the narratives they present to their local populations as well as to their government donors and political interlocutors. Fundraising narratives that show helpless people and media stories that only centre corruption, blaming people of colour in poorer countries, all contribute to the negative image of southern civil society. There are myriad ways to tell better stories that will ultimately penetrate people's imaginations. But its long game. The Pledge INGO signatories have committed to moving to storytelling that focuses on communities' strengths and successes, not what's wrong.

In the immediate term, policy needs to address not just the aspiration to get more funding to local CSOs, but the nitty gritty details that block the aspiration: auditing and tax rules, for example, and underlying procedures that enable grant-making to reach a wider net directly outside of OECD countries. Each bilateral donor in the OECD Development Assistance Committee (DAC) should do an audit of those rules that are in place that may be preventing DAC recommendations from being implemented – and make a commitment to eliminating at least the procedural barriers wherever possible.

The role of private philanthropy

In 2021, the Bill and Melinda Gates Foundation provided US$4.8 billion for global development projects. Putting this into perspective, this amount exceeds the Danish government's contribution to development, at $2.9 bn, and is roughly equal the size of Spain's or Switzerland's ODA budgets. The Gates Foundation's annual giving isn't far off the entire annual government budgets of Rwanda and Burkina Faso, at $4.2 billion and $5.3 billion, respectively.[63]

The influence of large sums of private philanthropy on development priorities is worrying. They can, for example, shape governments' priorities on how they spend their own budgets. The Gates Foundation, for example, has considerable investments (through, for example, the GAVI initiative[64]) in vaccines. In order for governments to get access to the funding, they often need to match fund. So, if Gates decides that malaria or vaccines are the public health priority, then governments often have no choice but to direct their own funding there if they want access to these funds.[65] Other public health issues – which might include clean water, or public health education – are no longer prioritized if they're not on the Gates' list.

Research shows how private philanthropy follows the flag of official government donors: the allocation of interests are largely in line with those of their governments. This begs the question about independence and shows just how politicized philanthropy can be, in turn politicizing INGOs too, through their giving.[66] There have been a few academic and journalistic attempts to critique philanthro-capitalism, as practised by the likes of Gates and Jeff Bezos. But these mega-givers aren't the only players in town – there are thousands of other philanthropic institutions, both large and small, shaping the funding food chain. But whether it's outsized donors like Gates or Bezos or the smaller funders, the overall practice of philanthropic power remains largely unreconstructed.

Thankfully, this is starting to change. Edgar Villanueva's groundbreaking book, *Decolonizing Wealth: Indigenous Wisdom to Heal Divides and Restore Balance*, shook the philanthropic world when it was published in 2018. Villanueva argues that not only has philanthropic wealth been derived from slavery and exploitation, it perpetuates it; he effectively challenged philanthropy's place, demonstrating how it was rooted in colonialism and how it reinforced the concept of white saviours, with white experts on one side and the poor and needy on the other. Villanueva paved the way for deep conversations across philanthropy about how foundations spend their money, and who gets to decide on how to spend it.[67]

Philanthropists, in general, are still very much challenged by the view that they should let go of power, and the conversation around decolonizing wealth is alive and kicking and no doubt will be for some years to come. But what philanthropy has yet to discuss in any depth at all is what the role of INGOs really should be, and, moreover, how they, too, underpin the maintenance of the neocolonial system. It's easy for philanthropists to offer a guaranteed annual operating grant to large INGOs, or to give significant large grants in one fell swoop (as per the Open Society Foundation grant, to the tune of US$100 million, to Human Rights Watch in 2010, specifically to grow their work abroad, or the more recent Bezos Earth Fund's grant to the World Wide Fund for Nature for work on climate change, also to the tune of $100 million).[68] It helps that philanthropic givers routinely sit on INGO boards and former INGO leaders regularly join the ranks of philanthropic staff members and boards alike. As much as activists criticize the revolving door between corporations and governments, a similar revolving door relationship prevails in philanthropy and INGOs too that rarely gets a nod of concern. Should it?

In part thanks to Villanueva, the conversations around localization have been growing in philanthropic circles, with more and more foundations looking to shift funding away from INGOs to local CSOs. And some are already moving from talk to action, like McKenzie Scott's largesse, which is generally provided through large grants with no strings attached, part of the growing movement of 'trust-based philanthropy'.[69] The Hewlett Foundation, for example, announced in 2021 that it was going to direct almost all of its funding in some departments to local CSOs. In the UK, the Lankelly Chase Foundation announced in 2023 that it would completely shut down and give away all of their funding to marginalized groups, including groups of colour, acknowledging their colonial past head-on.[70]

Shaheen Kassim-Lakha, from the Hilton Foundation, also suggests that philanthropy has a significant role to play in shifting the system overall, not just in their own practice, but in who and how they influence. 'There is a strong allyship role that foundations need to play', she says. 'The role of institutional funding is to invest in the things that individuals can't do ... individual givers will almost always prefer to invest in vaccines or water or something that they perceive as more tangible'. She offers an example: 'private philanthropy should also support those parts of the system that can change the system: like engaging and influencing bilateral and multilateral donors to be more equitable in selecting partners, or trying to ensure that the INGOs they give to also offer equal share of overheads to their partners'. Finally, she says, 'private philanthropy can influence the landscape for funding capacity strengthening not only of individual organizations but of the networks and compliance systems that the system needs in order to function'.

INGOs are funders too

I have anecdotally observed that many who work in INGOs are somewhat lacking in self-awareness. A few years ago, I convened a large, two-day meeting in Barcelona with philanthropists and INGOs on the subject of civic space. The INGOs present felt like fish out of water: 'we're not funders', they told me, as they huddled in the corner wondering why they were invited. Except that they are. The budgets of INGOs – and the funding that flows from them – are larger than many philanthropic organizations. And – in spite of calls to localize or decolonize and shrink – the fundraising power continues to grow. In 2022, the income from Plan International was €1.1 billion,[71] having doubled in the past decade, up from €535 million in 2010.[72] Save the Children International had an income in 2022 of $2.7 billion.[73]

Ask any leader of a national or sub-national CSO and they all put INGOs into the same category as any other funder. And as many INGOs move away from direct implementation roles, their role as funder becomes ever more obvious. Many already give a portion of their income through partnerships and sub-grants. Save the Children, for example, sub-grants roughly 20% of its total income. If organizations like Save the Children were classified as philanthropic organizations, they would be more commonly referred to as intermediaries (and very large ones at that), assuming the role of consolidating funding from others and redistributing them. I've never heard an INGO refer to itself as an intermediary or 'funder-mediary' (another phrase often heard in philanthropic circles), but that is nonetheless what they are.

One of the strongest arguments that funders tend to make when they push back against more local funding is the administrative concern about volume. They quite typically say 'we can't possibly manage grants to thousands of small organizations; it's just not possible'. They use this to justify giving through INGOs, arguing that it's more efficient. INGOs either act as simple 're-granters', passing on funds through parameters set by others, or they seek implementing partnerships, rarely on equal terms. With easy internet access and the capacity to respond to funders' reporting and risk requirements, INGOs cement their role as intermediaries of choice for most larger funders, public and private alike. So it's not just bilateral funders who prefer this method: The Jeff Bezos Foundation, for example, chose the World Resources Institute as its implementing partner for a new local climate fund, putting the well-funded INGO institution into a position of dispersing millions of dollars in South America and Africa and deciding on the parameters for that funding.[74]

There is a burgeoning sector, though, of 'intermediaries' from whom INGOs can learn. These organizations – like the Kenya Community Development Fund, or the African Women in Development Fund, or community foundations – do take on large funds from donors to distribute locally. But they're not just passing through funds and helping to manage risk for larger donors: they're building movements, connecting civil society 'horizontally', growing local giving, and playing an integral role for civil society as a whole. The community foundation movement, which has been at the heart of the #ShiftThePower movement, is one example of this: where community foundations play the role of intermediaries for larger donors, they can often adopt a more inclusive approach to using these funds, with local communities and local organizations having power over how funds come to be used and how they are invested in local communities. This was done in Zambia, for example, through the innovative Zambian Governance Foundation. However, even with its aspirations of shifting power, the community foundation movement is often bound by the usual requirements of reporting, due diligence, and managing risk.

A significant source of the largest INGO income comes from bilateral governments. Save the Children, for example, sees more than half of its income, at almost US$700 million per year, come directly from governments. At least some of this is expected to be given to partners. With this large volume of funding at their disposal, how INGOs offer up funding to others becomes paramount. Learning from other 'intermediaries', that is, those who are more rooted in their local communities, should be something that all INGOs consider, though they would have to persuade the powers that be – their donor governments – of the merits of more open giving. The problem, until now, is that INGOs have not generally been prepared to act as risk-guarantors, but instead have let the donor call the shots, as discussed in Chapter 4.

Private giving, however, is the single most substantial source of income for many INGOs. In the UK, it is estimated that the public contributed £10 billion over a five year period – or 40% – of total income.[75] This should be the lowest hanging fruit in providing the ability to be free of the restrictions imposed by larger donors.

As long as INGOs are securing large amounts of funds – either from governments or from their own local populations – they have the power to rapidly seek to decolonize how they fund partnerships and work with others. When Oxfam GB adopted a decolonization strategy in early 2023, one of the most controversial of the proposals was about who gets to keep core costs. 'A cynic would say that an INGO business model allows a parasitic overhead extraction, allowing you to keep money in your home country, while dispersing the leftovers to subcontracts', says Danny Sriskandarajah, former CEO of Oxfam GB, 'so a political economy based on the trickle-down approach proved to go to the heart of our business model'.

Oxfam GB's new strategy adopts the Pledge for Change approach, whereby the headquarters (HQ) agree to share overheads on the same proportion as all partners.[76] This may not sound revolutionary, but it is a rare gesture in INGOs, responding to what Humentum calls the 'starvation cycle', whereby grantees and partners aren't funded sufficiently to cover their admin or so-called overhead costs.[77] In some cases, INGOs are even more extractive of costs than funders. International Alert, for one, a UK-headquartered INGO, charges a 12% fee to their local offices when they raise funding directly. Here, the periphery is raising funds to prop up a northern HQ. Oxfam, however, is also now giving more of its unrestricted funding as long-term core funding to its partners, as opposed to the usual approach, which has tended towards annual contracts rather than multi-year grants.

However, even with shared overhead costs, the 'deciding' still arguably remains in Oxfam's hands. A far more radical approach has been piloted by Transform Trade and ADDAction, both medium-sized INGOs headquartered in the UK. They have both been modelling a more participatory grant-making approach that sees local organizations in the driving and leadership seat for funding decisions. This puts these organizations more closely in the funder space, rather than in the traditional NGO space.

There are multiple ways to let go of the deciding and doing, too. While the core of Transform Trade's work will remain in advocacy and facilitating access to markets by small producers, when they work with local partners, they want them to have unrestricted funds to do what they want with. They have set up a small fund for producers to do just that. 'In everything we do – be it grant-making, or advocacy support, or brokering relationships between producers and the market – we need to be led by our partner's priorities, and the support that they need, not what we think they need', says Charlotte Timson, the CEO of Transform Trade.

The role of the INGO of the future shouldn't be to make decisions about allocation and expenditure, but instead to facilitate groups coming together, and to leverage funds as an investor, providing training and mentorship, and securing capital. It's a complete shift away from projects and focuses instead on process, embodying in practice what it means to be a new-model INGO – one based on strong relationships, trust, and solidarity. 'Projects should be the output of relationships', says Mohammed Awal Alhassan from Norsaac, who is driving participatory grant-making in Ghana as a way of shifting power between funders, INGOs, and local organizations.

Given the significant financial resources at many INGOs' disposal, even without reforming the bilateral or philanthropic relationship, there is a huge opportunity to engage the available resources in ways to shift power and invest in those groups who are much more locally rooted: providing core, unrestricted funding, enabling decision-making to happen at the local level, and supporting their efforts to raise capital on their own terms.

The private sector: The elephant in the room?

The private sector is a growing actor in international spaces and is often supplanting civil society's role, especially in areas of service delivery. Some argue that if international civil society steps out of the space of direct delivery, the private sector will just move in, taking us even further away from the localization agenda. And you can see this anecdotally – in hindsight. The UK government used to have programme partnership agreements (PPAs) with major INGOs. Each partnership was worth millions of dollars in guaranteed core income for the likes of the WWF, Christian Aid, Save the Children, and many others.[78] PPAs were the mainstay enshrining the dominant role of INGOs in the bilateral funding space. After PPAs were abolished in 2016, there was an immediate growth in private sector spending.

In the last 10 years, the role of the private sector as contractors to aid agencies has grown considerably. One estimate shows that in 2021, as much as 25% of USAID spending, about US$5 billion, was contracted through the private sector, much of this to large international companies, like Deloitte, PwC, and Chemonics. Some 340 individual companies are listed as USAID implementers.[79] Sometimes referred to as 'Beltway Bandits', they yield significant influence politically in order to secure government contracts.

Although a seemingly smaller portion of aid funding was spent through the private sector in the UK – about 4% in 2021 – the figure gets significantly higher when we look at in-country spending, with an additional 14% being spent through private sector companies. Some, like Adam Smith International, act as new intermediaries for government, managing money on the Foreign, Commonwealth and Development Office's behalf, either through INGOs, local organizations, or other private sector subcontractors.[80]

What does this mean for our shifting power agenda and the role of INGOs? For some in local civil society, it simply means building new partnerships outside of the INGO space. Especially where local private sector companies are involved – and expenditure here also has the potential to grow – there is an alliance against the hegemony of INGOs as their partner of choice. This is particularly relevant for community-led projects in areas such as renewable energy or agriculture. But it can also lead to bias, with funding more available for certain types of programmes. 'Impact investing' for example – a growing buzzword in philanthropic circles – certainly leads to funding that leads to prejudice against projects that aren't scalable, or that don't have a potential income source. The result is the defacto privatization of public services: health, education, and more.

There is certainly a risk that, as USAID and others increase their aim to spend locally, they will choose what they perceive as the most efficient, larger actor, aka the Beltway Bandits. Justin Sandefur, from the Centre for Global Development, has encouraged more direct giving from bilateral donors to states to increase accountability.[81] This could be a risk for local civil society, which may end up taking an even smaller share of international investment than it does now.

Advocacy, human rights, or other civil society needs most certainly won't come via private sector sources. From a shifting power perspective, this is worrying: if the civil society models have an immediate private sector bias, then there is even less core funding for local civil society. Decisions will be made by international actors, now with a private sector identity, unlikely to share values, voice, or power.

Given the rising role of the private sector, there are three responses: one is to ignore them entirely and get better at demonstrating the value of civil society overall. The second response is to bring the private sector into the conversation, but find ways to hold it to account in the same way as we're asking other actors in the international system to do. One example of this is the 'Equity Index',[82] which was first tested on the UK development consultancy sector, in part acknowledging that there's more to international actors than INGOs – and to encourage their direct role in shifting power. And there is a current drive to engage civil society more directly in standards setting for financial markets.[83] Indeed, inclusion and shifting power are key drivers helping to contribute solutions in multiple areas.

INGOs and others can also embrace some of the private sector approaches, such as investing in social enterprises. The Zambian Governance Foundation, though not an INGO, did just this by creating Chaluka in 2017, a social enterprise offering local investment in energy, agriculture, and environmental projects.[84] Social enterprise models may not reach all parts of society, and rely on the ability to provide a return – so they are not necessarily appropriate models for all that civil society does. But they are a way of moving away from traditional funding sources and building reliance and sustainability.

Finally, INGOs also need to continuously reflect on their specific role as a counterbalance to private sector influence and power more closely. This doesn't necessarily mean delivering programmes or services as a competitor to the private sector, but playing a similar role to the one they might do towards government: acting in solidarity with local civil society, and holding international actors, including the private sector, to account. Many INGOs already do this in a range of areas –human rights, trade justice, environment, and more – but it's rarely a core area of work. Indeed, many INGOs shy away from corporate accountability as they see the private sector as donors, or potential donors, to their cause. But INGOs have the ability to help connect dots between different countries, to look at patterns of behaviour and common threads to paint a picture of what's happening, and to help amplify what local actors want and need from the private sector as a whole. They can ensure that funding that is going to the private sector is fair and equitable, includes local voices, and measures up to social or environmental justice ambitions. They can also ensure that funding going to the private sector isn't being diverted at the expense of what can and should be done by local civil society actors.

***

Ultimately, most CSOs would prefer not to be beholden to funders, or at least would prefer to be in the driver's seat. Adeso, the African-based organization working in Kenya, Somalia, and Sudan, led by Degan Ali, is seeking a clear line of independence from funders. Having already eschewed government funding years before – as it came with too many strings attached and put into question its local legitimacy – the organization was reliant on philanthropy and INGO partners. With no previous unrestricted funding, upon receiving a US$5 million unrestricted grant from MacKenzie Scott in 2022, Adeso proceeded to use the funds to leverage its independence, investing in profit-making activity (such as real estate and a water company), rather than using it to underpin its annual operating costs. Its ambition is now to grow a $50 million endowment within 10 year's time to support the organization's work. If successful, this would be a complete game changer, not just for Adeso, but as a model for many other organizations too, who are currently relying on the trickle-down approach to funding. All donors, whether governments, philanthropists, or INGOs, could feasibily create investment support for local CSOs for this type of future independence.

In 2022, the RINGO Project initiated a trial to re-engineer the ways in which local organizations engage with the international funding sector, through piloting the idea of a 'reverse call for proposals'. The current practice of grant-making is generally to issue calls for applications, or to invite groups to apply for funding. INGOs often issue calls for proposals for implementing partners for various pots of funds for projects that were either initiated by them or from donor-derived funding. What became known as the RINGO Alternative Solidarity Model posited that local civil society groups could come together and collectively identify their needs and in turn issue a 'reverse call' for proposals to the international sector, aimed at INGOs and traditional funders alike. The reverse call would seek out financial support and support in kind. The ambition is that the reverse call for proposals could become the standard practice for receiving international funding or in building INGO and local organizations' relationships in the future. There are challenges with this approach, in practice, as local organizations need funding to convene to get to this stage, and funders need the mechanisms and processes to respond. But at least the ideas aren't being driven by someone sitting in an office in Washington, DC or London.

INGOs continue to promote their own self-interest by dominating access to funders. And it's not in their survival interests to let go, either. The RINGO Project's initial inquiry report confirmed the deep-rootedness of a privileged unwillingness, whereby white people are simply unwilling to give up their power. Giving up, for example, the precious guaranteed funding offered from bilateral partnership agreements is like turkeys voting for Christmas. But with the intention of creating a more equitable civil society, the turkeys do indeed have to start voting for Christmas.

From a demand perspective, Moses Isooba, from the Uganda National NGO Forum, and a master of words, says fervently: 'we do not need tools, that is the paracetamol approach. The paracetamol approach just maintains the status quo'. Instead, he argues, 'we need the "vaccine approach", a longer-term commitment in finding a cure to ensure the survival and sustainability of stronger civil societies everywhere. Dose 1: direct funding; dose 2: unrestricted funding; and dose 3 (booster dose): multi-year funding. The vaccine approach takes us from rhetoric to action'.

Across all of the funding sectors – official donors, philanthropy, and INGOs – the vaccine approach could be the antidote we need. Rightly or wrongly, funders are the masters of the universe. They have a helicopter view of the system, and they have the ability to support it, to co-design, and to transform it. There are inherent risks associated with this level of power, but private philanthropy can take those risks and provide the proof of concept that the 'vaccines' can work, enabling others – like bilateral funders, who have a different approach to risk – to follow.

CHAPTER SIX
Knowledge is power

In the late 1990s, it was considered enlightened to talk about the 'beneficiaries' of aid. In fact, the Ombudsman Project at the British Red Cross had a functioning strap-line: 'accountability to the beneficiaries of aid'. Today, it's no longer an acceptable phrase. It's both pejorative and patronizing, implying complete passivity on the part of the people INGOs are working with. New phrases have emerged, like 'constituencies' or even 'rights holders' or 'co-investors', implying those that INGOs are working with are not a charitable burden, but rather people to whom we have a genuine accountability.

Those of us who are born and raised English speakers are often oblivious to the issue of language. In fact, we're not just oblivious, but arrogant: it's assumed that anyone working in an international setting will speak English. But looking at language turned out to be central to the work of the RINGO Project. This was perceived to be as critical as looking at operational systems, risk and accountability, or other areas of change. 'Ultimately, all of our change in shifting power is about relationships', says Moses Isooba of the Uganda National NGO Forum, 'and language is how we communicate in a relationship. We ring-fence people who get paid in development by using a coded language. We don't want the other people to speak. We speak in acronyms, frameworks, but they're veils, they mask the real human beings like you and me, and if we can change the language, we can build better relationships.'

Language is power: it can reinforce old stereotypes, drive unfair power dynamics and maintain roles around different actors in the system. Or it can create an equal footing – a meeting place of equals. By changing our language, and questioning the words we use, and how we use them, we can have a much more powerful interrogation of the work that we do and how we work in solidarity with others. Here is one key example: think of the phrase 'poor countries'. If we adjust that to say 'impoverished countries', we immediately reveal a key question about perpetrators: people aren't poor because they're not clever or because they're lazy; there was an active hand in stealing resources through colonialism or unfair economic systems.

Language, nonetheless, is a minefield. It's constantly evolving and modernizing, with new words seeping into everyday usage and old words becoming no longer acceptable. In the RINGO Project, phrases like 'the field', 'empowerment', or 'developing countries' were all more or less maligned for various reasons. The field was identified as a disparaging generalization, harking back to safari-capped white upper class English men in the 1930s going out to 'the field' in colonial times ('mission' has a similar connotation, although it's still acceptable for people in some INGOs or the United Nations to go on 'mission' – harking back to the missionaries seeking to convert 'the natives'). 'Empowerment' implies that someone has no power or that people lack agency; 'developing countries', meanwhile, implies a hierarchy between nations that pejoratively suggests backwardness.

As part of our journey on rebuilding INGOs, our language – and sources of knowledge – need to be made more equitable too. We need to reinvent the language so as to remove old hints of colonialism, in line with the decolonization agenda. Right now, the dominant colonial languages – English, French, or Spanish – are always the meeting point, whether you speak Luganda (a local language in Uganda), Arabic, or Filipino. The sector's jargon is generally in English, with many words not even translating into other languages at all: accountability, for example, a common phrase in the sector, doesn't even translate readily into Latin languages.

So often, international actors centre the use of our language in the western world, not in the constituencies with whom we are engaging. We undertake, for example, 'capacity building' (we're the ones with the know-how, local people have no knowledge) or we provide aid (generously gifting from our own hands, rather than providing reparations for assets stolen, or solidarity in sharing the world's resources). We expect people in communities to speak our language, and use our jargonistic phrases, and make little effort to enable people to communicate in their own words, jargon-free.

The practicality of language

The fact that most funders operate largely in English places an undue burden on local actors. Small civil society organizations (CSOs) operating in non-English-speaking countries would necessarily have to retain English-speaking expertise to access funders. They need to have knowledge of the language and the jargon used, even if the work they're seeking funding for is rooted locally. Rasha Sansur, a communication and resource mobilization adviser who speaks English and Arabic and works in Palestine, told me:

> Development is a postcolonial construct and all of the language used was originally developed in English. So I would only ever write a funding application or an evaluation in English. If I use Arabic – even if the funder allows me to – it won't include the phrases they need to hear to pass the funding bar. It needs to include the 'flow' expected by English speakers: goals, mission, outcomes, etc ... even though we might personally address things differently in our culture.

This is the reason why the signatories of the Pledge for Change have embedded the issue of language and communication into their commitments. They have committed to end the use of jargon that can't be easily translated into many languages, for example, alongside committing to use authentic storytelling that centres communities' strengths rather than what they don't have. It's a solid starting point. But haven't we been here before?

Déjà vu?

There have been many attempts in recent years to formally address the issue of language. Both Bond, the UK network of international development agencies, and Partos, the Dutch network, have undertaken studies and working groups to address the issue of language.[85] The former looked specifically at the language emerging from the UK government and helpfully addresses the colonial undertones, suggesting the sector avoid similar language, including phrases like 'Global Britain' or 'British values'. A 2018 study by Intrac also looked at the issue and offered some practical suggestions about how to build sensitivity into language for both INGOs and donors alike. These included quite obvious things like ensuring budgeting for technical skills to ensure culturally sensitive translation and ensuring that evaluation systems take account of cultural and linguistic differences.[86]

Why then, are we still talking about this some years later? Because language sits firmly in the category of culture – and culture change doesn't happen overnight, especially when it's mixed with power. I'm still listening to the music I grew up with in the 1980s even though my 21-year-old son mocks my musical choices for being old-fashioned and outdated. We resist change because it takes us out of our comfort zone. And perhaps nowhere more than the issue of language in INGOs does it start to become uncomfortable. As a consequence, action on changing language is easily dismissed as being less important than other things.

When Moses Isooba worked for Danida in Uganda, where he was referred to as 'the local', the issue of language was constantly dismissed when challenged:

> My Danish colleague would use the word 'stupid', which in my context is abusive. For her, it simply meant false. I suggested she use a different word because we were in Uganda, not Denmark, and she simply brushed it aside. Her language – be it English or Danish – always took priority over our cultural sensitivity. She didn't like being challenged.

If enough people start to think about change, change happens – so being sensitive to language could be the ideal starting point on a shifting power journey. We need to rapidly start using the phrases that can redefine our power relationships in international civil society and be sensitive to language when challenged. If someone says 'that word is offensive', it's not very difficult to stop using it and find another term, even if you've been using it for 25 years. And there are many tools out there that help with this, from the Bond tool to the RINGO lexicon.[87]

In addition to using different terminology, we also need to make more of an effort to invest in translation. Translation is often an afterthought, something that falls by the wayside when the funding is scarce. And let's be honest – it's difficult to work through translators, especially in the online world where most of us work these days. It slows you down, it can be clunky and not always accurate, and it makes conversation more, rather than less, formal. But that doesn't justify our ongoing de-prioritization of it, either. If we treat translation not as an afterthought (and I'm certainly guilty of this), but instead as central to shifting power – as core to accessibility and to removing barriers – then it should be embedded in almost everything we do.

For written communication, things should be much simpler, as the opportunity presented by artificial intelligence should remove so many barriers to language. Online translation tools are more accessible than ever, and increasingly use indigenous languages too. At the time of writing, Google Translate offered 133 languages, from Luganda, to Pashto, to Malayalam. Enabling partners to offer written communication in their own language – whatever it might be – would make things easier for others and reduce significant barriers to engagement. There are small risks of using corporate tools like Google, especially for sensitive human rights work, but most work in civil society that people want to communicate in writing can be done this way: emails, grant applications, evaluations, research, and more.

More than just words

It's not just the words we use, it's how we use them. INGOs are notorious for their use of storytelling that centres people as victims in need of help. Marketing materials and advocacy materials all rely on our heart strings being pulled, framing those we work with as victims in order to garner support.

Africa No Filter shines a light on the narratives that have become so embedded in the stories that are told about the continent: stories shaped by colonial writers, like Joseph Conrad, right through to modern day 'saviours', like Bono and Bob Geldof. Famous films like Leonard DiCaprio's *Blood Diamond* or the *Kony 2012* viral documentary all reinforce and perpetuate old stereotypes and singular negative narratives.[88]

Rose Caldwell, the CEO of Plan International and a signatory to the Pledge for Change, writes, '[w]e start by acknowledging that sometimes the stories we tell as INGOs can, inadvertently, reinforce harmful stereotypes. We must recognize that even when we want to show the harsh realities of poverty, conflict and hunger, we have a responsibility to do so in a way that does not exploit people or portray them as helpless victims'.[89] Instead, like other signatories, Plan International has pledged to put local people at the centre of the story, and let them set the terms of the story they want to tell. As Caldwell writes, '[w]e'll amplify the stories people want to tell rather than merely speaking [sic] on their behalf'.

The prioritization of knowledge

The language we use is how we express the knowledge we have, too. Thus, part of the effort to create a new and more inclusive language is to peel back the layers and understand where the production of knowledge in INGO work comes from. And formal knowledge that underpins most work in the sector, be it academic, INGO, or think-tank led, unsurprisingly has an acute bias towards western ideas, further reinforcing the binary of what Moses Isooba refers to as 'ivory tower knowledge versus ebony tower knowledge'.

Enrique Mendizabal, the founder of On Think Tanks, which compiles open data on think tanks and their funding, examined the resources of think tanks, looking at issues in the majority world and their geographic origin.[90] What he found was unsurprising: that the bulk of funding available for research on Africa, Asia, and Latin America is awarded to researchers in Europe and North America.

> Picture this scenario: researchers based in a remote German village are awarded a significant sum of money to investigate and find solutions to the challenges faced by the United States' (US') primary education sector. The principal researchers in the project are well-regarded in their field. They spent a year collecting data in North Dakota during their graduate studies and have visited the US frequently over the years – but they have never lived there. Yet, they are given millions of dollars to explore the complex challenges faced by students, parents, educators and communities across the entire US. Needless to say, the American researchers are not happy about this. They reach out to the funder to complain and argue that, if anyone should be studying the US, it should be them.[91]

In this scenario that Mendizabal relays, most would agree with the American researchers. Yet this is exactly what happens in international work. If we don't think it makes sense in the US education sector, why do we think it makes sense in the context of international development, human rights, or conservation?

The wealthiest think tanks 'serving' the development and environment community are still based in London and Washington, DC: the Overseas Development Institute, the Centre for Global Development, the International Institute for Environment and Development, and many more. Although many are now staffed by diverse academics, the production of knowledge comes from calls for proposals that originate in Europe or North America. Even with a growing list of academic institutions located outside of Europe or North America, these institutions, too, are still the dominant actors in knowledge production for development and environment.

Whose knowledge counts?

Anyone who has worked in or studied international development in the last few decades should be familiar with Robert Chambers' work: 'putting the first last' and 'putting the last first'. The mantra rose in popularity in the 1990s after the academic, then working for the World Bank, championed the idea that INGOs, or indeed the wider international system, weren't the ones best placed to identify the needs of local people. It now seems a no-brainer that local people should be involved in some programme decision-making.[92]

But Chambers' approach, although revolutionary at the time, still kept decision-making power around knowledge production in the hands of donors and INGOs. It was a mechanism to engage local people, but not necessarily one to shift power. We have long paid little more than lip service to indigenous and local knowledge across the INGO sector.

This isn't unique to INGOs, of course; it is endemic in society. The phrase 'first generation learner' – often applied to people who are the first to go through formal education in their family – is indicative of this phenomenon. It intrinsically dismisses the knowledge of those without formal education or who may be illiterate. Farmers, grandmothers, even small business owners – if they didn't receive formal education, their knowledge is deemed unworthy. While INGO systems have been increasingly seeking to source knowledge from indigenous communities, our processes are rarely set up to centre these forms of knowledge in our work. Participation in a funder or INGO strategy process, for example, may involve sourcing background papers from researchers, or having a series of 'experts' present their knowledge in a board meeting, or recruiting a 'high-level advisory panel'. The knowledge of local people, however, is three steps removed from such a process. Access isn't there and we assume they would lack the ability to synthesize their knowledge in a way that helps us build our strategies.

The assumption that knowledge is centred in the North is so ingrained in our work that it reinforces the patterns of power in the international system. 'I think one of the biggest challenges we have is to counteract this idea that knowledge has to come from somewhere and be transferred to us', says Charles Kojo van Dyck of the West Africa Civil Society Institute. 'We have indigenous knowledge here and experience. If we're looking at a global civil society or going beyond colonialism, we should be looking at how do we actually share and exchange this knowledge and not just the idea knowledge from the Global South doesn't even exist or isn't recognized'.[93]

One study on the history of the humanitarian system referred to the fact that while building knowledge and expertise was, and continues to be, important, its western-centrism has set the patterns in the sector for decades. The study cites an illustrative humanitarian worker who said 'we used to read the new development manuals at night and then teach the villagers what we learned the next day'. The authors write: '[i]n this way, Western workers' training and education contributed to their sense that they were justified in intervening in the "best interests" of those affected by conflict or disasters, and that "science was on their side". Making the humanitarian community more open to 'outsider' knowledge has been and remains a very challenging task'.[94] That was in 2013. I'm not sure that we're much further along.

Everything from global campaign priorities to organizational strategies are agreed and designed by people usually sitting in Europe or North America, where language excludes people and knowledge from elsewhere can be marginalized.

In 2013, a small group of UK-based INGO campaign veterans from Make Poverty History – a hugely successful 2005 global campaign for international debt relief – launched a revival, this time called the IF campaign. IF was an anti-hunger campaign, meant to recapture the spirit of Make Poverty History. By this time, populism was on the rise, following the 2008–09 economic crisis, and interest in international development was waning everywhere.

At the time, I was working on a campaign to end speculation on food commodities with the UK-based movement-led organization the World Development Movement (now Global Justice Now), alongside activists in the global food sovereignty movement from across Latin America, Africa, and Asia. Our work was both deeply researched and coordinated with the food sovereignty movement. Collectively, we had identified speculation by financiers in London and New York as one of the major reasons behind food poverty. Our policy analysis wasn't included in any of the policy demands of the IF campaign at this point.

I called up one of the INGOs involved to see what could be done, and was firmly told: 'we haven't decided if this is an issue'. I asked about their consultation process with local organizations and the person I spoke to said bluntly: 'we haven't consulted', and furthermore that 'if you sign up to the IF campaign, you sign up to our policy recommendations, you can't add anything in'. In other words, 'we have the knowledge, we decide on what's important'. The IF campaigners ultimately added in food speculation as an issue, after doing their own work, and duplicating ours. A year later, when we won huge legislative change at the EU level, the large organization I spoke to and the IF campaign claimed full credit.

There are times when we need academic and international expertise on issues, and some of this will indeed come from academics in the US, the UK, or elsewhere in OECD countries. In the case of speculation in food commodities, we needed people with insight and expertise into how commodity trading worked, and into the US and European regulatory systems; these experts were naturally based in New York, Washington, DC, London, and Brussels. But this 'expert' knowledge was coupled with significant knowledge from local people about how they experienced food price spikes, and the wider food sovereignty movement about whether or not they wanted this issue to be a focus of a northern-led campaign.

Shifting power would seem to require a whole shift in where we source our knowledge from, and, to go deeper, the decision-making that surrounds the use of knowledge, too.

A new language centring knowledge in communities

A new language is already emerging that challenges the power dynamic so central in the international system. The Global Fund for Community Foundations likes to talk about 'assets' rather than 'charity'. Instead of looking at the communities and their so-called 'charitable' needs, it first identifies the 'assets' that communities already have – knowledge, spaces, tools, and more – and asks for people to invest more in their development. They minimize the focus on what people don't have, and instead start from a position of what they do have; this makes constituents active, rather than passive, actors in their own development.

Academic or technical knowledge centred in institutions outside of the west need far more attention and investment. A think-tank initiative led by the International Development Research Centre has invested US$200 million over 10 years, for example, to build African think tanks.[95] The programme, however, closed in 2019. Are there sustainable sources of funding? How are the major think tanks, from the Brookings Institute, to the ODI, looking at their own efforts to shift power? Are INGOs making a stronger effort to find knowledge from researchers and academics outside of the UK, US, and Europe? Can we start with pairing academics from different contexts and continents when research is being sourced?

Perhaps more importantly, how can we embrace the knowledge in local communities in ways that aren't tokenistic at best, or pejorative at worst? How can we ensure that knowledge is genuinely built to be inclusive? Robert Chambers tried this almost three decades ago, but we don't seem to have moved much further along.

Talk To Loop, an initiative that uses digital tools to engage people, is, in its own words, 'transforming how humanitarian and development organizations learn from the communities they work with'.[96] Because of the advent of digital technology, the system can enable feedback, input, and many other forms of interaction and engagement with local people – in whatever language they choose. It doesn't have to be in written form, either, freeing up people from 'the tyranny of translation'. People can use whatever platform they prefer too, from Facebook, to WhatsApp, to Telegram.

While Loop is essentially a digital accountability mechanism, the fact that people can communicate in their own language is central. 'I used to be Director of Programmes and Partnership at the British

Red Cross', says Alex Ross, Loop's founder, continuing:

> I was getting more and more uncomfortable making
> decisions on behalf of others. We weren't listening to
> communities, they weren't in the lead. I didn't speak the
> local language and I don't understand their culture and
> context. We were paying for advisers to go out and assess
> communities – and they didn't speak the language either.
> It was absurd. So, through Loop, we enable people to
> communicate in their language, and anonymously if need
> be, which means we are shifting power in a much more
> direct way, giving people agency to speak up, to participate
> more directly in shaping our work, or hold us to account.
> We couldn't do this 20 years ago, but we can now, thanks
> to digital technology.

Sometimes, change can start at the top

Governance systems of INGOs, as discussed in Chapter 3, are ripe
for reform, and they are a central place in which to embed new ways
of sourcing knowledge. If the governance of an organization rejects
old language and embraces a new lexicon, it sets the tone for the
rest of the organization: new narratives and authentic storytelling
will follow. How the organization presents itself internally and to
the outside world should be fully aligned.

Boards equally need to be more interactive with the communities
they serve. Based on the findings of a 2023 survey about what local
CSOs want, the West Africa Civil Society Institute urged boards to
engage in the locally led development movement, with the number
one priority being to foster a continuous learning environment and
open culture.[97]

Breaking down the barriers of language, ensuring input from
communities is not merely tokenistic. Centring their knowledge
and language in strategic discussions about organizational direction
– or, to put it simply, being open – are part of fostering this type
of environment. Talk To Loop is one way to do this: getting direct
input and feedback on issues that are impacting the communities
where INGOs work, and amplifying these stories too. Equally
important is formalizing relationships with experts based outside of
the ivory towers of Washington, DC or London, and to give regular,

honest, and insightful guidance into the strategy and direction of any organization, investing in building the capacity of indigenous knowledge centres in Africa, Asia, and Latin America.

To shift power, we need to embrace a new culture of openness and a new culture of language, and reject the notion that those of us who may have only worked in an INGO, or studied development, or are employed in philanthropy, have more knowledge than those who experience first-hand the conditions where they live on how to effect change. Finding ways to enable this knowledge to come to the fore in organizations is paramount.

CHAPTER SEVEN
Breaking it down, sector by sector

I've had the privilege of being able to work across many issues in and with the INGO sector since the late 1990s. Thus, I've seen the good, the bad, and the ugly across each and every one of the sectors I've engaged with in the past 25 years: the humanitarian and development sectors, human rights, and the environment sector.

The RINGO Project is intentionally cross-sector. The issues impacting INGOs affect almost all organizations, regardless of the issue they work on: decolonization, gender, structural racism, risk, funding, power – all of the issues addressed in this book. And the demands from many civil society organizations (CSOs) working at the national or local levels are also universal: more bottom-up power and increased, more ethical forms of localization. Nonetheless, each sector has its particular nuance that it contends with. This chapter takes a slightly more granular look at the issues as they impact organizations working in different INGO sectors.

The humanitarian and development sectors

In my first role in the aid sector, working with the British Red Cross, I have a vivid memory of a desk officer for the Balkans bemoaning the fact that a war had broken out (Kosovo) and he was stuck at a desk in London while other colleagues got to 'do the *real* stuff of delivering aid to the poor refugees'. Though he was educated at Eton, the same British private school where prime ministers and royal family members also get their education, he didn't see the irony in his comments – or, for that matter, recognize his privilege. It was one of my earliest exposures to 'white saviourism' and something that drew me away from the work of humanitarians.

This was in 1998. At the time, the general practice was: an emergency broke out; money was raised in a wide appeal; resources, both financial and human, were secured and people would fly out to the crisis and set up whatever response was required: refugee camps, emergency supplies, and, in the case of war, someone (white, western-educated) to negotiate safe passage for those caught up in the conflict. Local organizations may have worked with international actors, but they were usually the local branch of the INGO rather than genuinely local actors. On the ground, before federations were consolidated, the local INGO would have to navigate the complexity of relationships with their international counterparts, often with separate local staff. In one country, the local chapter of the INGO would have separate relationships with affiliates in the US, the UK, France, etc.

To a degree, things have shifted since these early days of my career. And certainly for the past five years or more, the notion of locally led development, at least in theory, has been at the centre of many conversations. The idea of 'decolonizing development', however, still remains relatively new. In fact, a conference in 1955 saw development, and presumably the development sector, as decolonizing in itself. At this conference, development was seen as 'the liberatory human aspiration to attain freedom from political, economic, ideological, epistemological and social domination that occurred under colonialism and coloniality'.[98] But decolonization in the sector now largely includes the idea of abolishing white saviourism, and eradicating the idea that countries need to 'develop' along traditional western models.

For most critiques referred to in this book, the humanitarian sector was in the firing line before others. I've already touched on most of the pertinent issues impacting the sector directly, from the sexual exploitation scandals of 2018 (see Chapter 4), to the 2016 Grand Bargain commitments (see Chapter 5), which recognizes the absurdity of sending westerners to deliver aid when there is a rich resource of local actors who are already doing the bulk of the work, but with limited resources. It may have been the first global recognition of the need to shift at least some of the power and privilege away from INGOs (and multilaterals, like the United Nations [UN]).

International development was always about the narrative and practice of the west coming to 'develop' the majority world, with an assumption that good development was based on a western liberal model of economics, society, and governance. Arguably, sustainable development models should have challenged this assumption: they unpack the folly of unfettered economic growth and its links to climate change and acknowledge that our models of so-called 'development' in the west are putting the world in peril. But efforts in this arena have still failed to overturn the dominance of western-dominated approaches in humanitarian and development work led by INGOs, despite some governments proactively rejecting even seemingly apolitical humanitarian INGOs from operating in their territory, as Indonesia did following a tsunami in 2018.[99]

Some further key issues that have emerged from those who challenge the dominance of western approaches in the humanitarian and development sector are relevant to highlight here. First is the concept of 'neutrality', embedded into international humanitarian law. The work of humanitarian actors, in particular, has always hidden behind the façade of political neutrality. The Red Cross movement is at the heart of this, arguing that the only way that they can secure help for victims of war is by being able to negotiate with both sides of a conflict, and often with both perpetrators and victims alike. While this may seem reasonable from their standpoint, this principle has also found its way into agreements with all civil society actors seeking international funding, and those working with INGOs on the ground have argued that this is a significant barrier to their ability to receive funding. Ukrainian organizations, for example, may choose a different path, wanting to support their troops with food or medical help. For this, they are denied funding.

Neutrality is a complex issue when seen in the light of shifting power. When actors on the ground are increasingly demanding solidarity, whether it's an extreme case of war, or economic solidarity, arguing against inequality or corruption, neutrality may be a difficult act to balance. INGOs will revert to the easier charitable causes that mask the political nature of their work. Who can argue, for example, with such laudable causes as vaccinations, education, or providing clean drinking water? But the lack of these things is, in itself, a political choice. INGOs that remain 'neutral' and offer to fill these gaps through charitable work and, for example, by letting go of work around human rights to satisfy a country host, may be aiding and abetting – directly or indirectly – governments or other actors who fail to serve populations.

Who should humanitarian or development actors take the lead from in terms of steering their work? How do they make decisions about what their role and offering is? Continuing to help local populations is a strong driver, but making these decisions from London or Washington, DC, or Geneva is ignorant of the real needs and desires of local actors and the political drivers at play. Even when humanitarian actors have ceded to the demands of repressive and autocratic regimes, we've seen a growing number of attacks on humanitarian actors in recent years and even criminalization: neutrality is no longer a guarantee of access or safety. The work of humanitarianism and development is political. We can't ignore that. Charitable neutrality is something that INGOs working in development and humanitarian action should question head-on. This will have implications about how they work, and about funding sources in particular.

This isn't to say that all development is neutral. International debt relief campaigns, led by the development sector, faced up squarely to the fact that countries weren't poor: in fact, they were 'impoverished' by western models of development finance (debt). Global campaigns on inequality and tax justice are similarly political. Nonetheless, many INGOs continue to develop programmes framed squarely in the charitable space, ignoring the political role of western actors, and indeed the demands from local actors.

As highlighted in earlier chapters, the humanitarian sector has been at the forefront of arguments around shifting power. In some ways, those in the sector have the most to shift and transform in order to be locally led. This means that institutions in the sector have the most to lose in terms of funding, influence or direct staffing; but, putting it another way, they also have the most to contribute to the transformation.

The environment sector

In 2021, Extinction Rebellion (XR) activists targeted World Wide Fund for Nature (WWF) UK's offices in Woking, accusing the world's largest environmental organization of mass evictions of indigenous peoples in Kenya, and of aiding and abetting the world's top polluters, in spite of the organization's stated mission. This isn't the first time WWF has been called out. In 2019, it was accused of colluding with paramilitaries and harming local communities in the name of conservation in Nepal and the Democratic Republic of the Congo. This was backed up by a UN investigation, finding that WWF had caused serious harm and trauma to local populations. An investigation by an independent panel, appointed by WWF, found the organization's own practices to have not met international human rights standards.[100]

The environmental movement isn't radically different from other INGO sectors, but it hasn't necessarily faced the reckoning that other INGO sectors have to date, despite the occasional scandal that hits the headlines. If there have been any conversations about decolonization or shifting power, they have remained well below the radar.

Whatever the rights and wrongs of environmental activists, like XR calling out other environmental activists, it presents an ongoing challenge for many in the environment movement trying to bridge the politics of right and left, which is a common positioning of organizations working in the conservation sector. Indigenous communities and local activists, nonetheless, have rightly pointed out that the conservation model favoured by big environmental NGOs (ENGOs) is flawed: it can restrict access to ancestral lands, treating local communities as the enemy of conservation, in spite of significant evidence to the contrary.

ENGOs can also supplant indigenous and local voices on the international stage, though often unwittingly, such as at the Glasgow climate talks in 2022, where many local actors were prevented from attending either due to unaffordability or, in some cases, unnecessary quarantine measures as a result of the COVID-19 pandemic.[101] To overcome this barrier, there needs to be deliberate and considerable effort by the predominantly white, northern ENGOs to take a back stage and enable local and indigenous groups to be at the forefront on the international stage. Greenpeace, for one, have issued an internal policy statement on how it intends to work with indigenous people, following some criticism they faced at the Paris climate talks in 2015.[102]

The 'saving animals' approach to conservation can also fail to address root causes of biodiversity loss or climate change, instead supporting often-contested solutions and short-term fixes, such as sustainable palm oil. But these decisions are made by staff and board members whose history is embedded in western business models and western approaches. Fundraising models, meanwhile, reinforce western capitalism, often seeing ENGOs aligned with companies (from banks to supermarkets) in large corporate partnerships. When I worked at WWF, a colleague used to joke how we 'stamped the panda on any corporate ass that'll give us money'. This can have seriously devastating effects, too, sometimes silencing INGOs into submission in order to satisfy a corporate donor, as happened recently in the case of WWF and its relationship with a major supermarket, Tesco, around the company's pollution of a major river in the UK.[103]

Most ENGOs have been created in the North and their governance remains firmly rooted there. And while many have made inroads in diversifying their boards in terms of colour or race, their systems still remain dominated by western approaches and western values. Structural racism weighs heavily on the environment sector. It doesn't help that the sector lacks diversity. Indeed, a comprehensive study in the UK found that only about 1 in 20 workers in the environmental charity sector identified as an ethnic minority in 2023.[104]

The 'whiteness' of the sector is further reinforced by the stories the media tells. Many will recall how the photo of a young Ugandan activist, Vanessa Nakate, was cropped out of an image with white activist Greta Thunberg at Davos in 2020.[105]

We prefer to highlight the work of famous white saviours over local actors, giving the impression that only rich white people from the west can save the environment: David Attenborough, or actor Emma Thompson, or even King Charles, when he was still a lowly prince. Perhaps this is why the 'great and the good' are readily available to pitch in to environmental causes. Conservation International boasts actor Harrison Ford and fashion designer Stella McCartney among their board members, and who can forget the work of Sting and his wife Trudie Styler to 'save the Amazon'?[106] [107] This is not to diminish their role, but it is recognizing how celebrities, rather than the many thousands of others who have worked tirelessly on environmental matters for decades, are celebrated.

Environmental causes are popular for people to support, and they often cross the political spectrum. This means that the largest brands bring in considerable sums of money. In 2020, the income for WWF Worldwide approached the US$1 billion mark, at €888 million.[108] In that same year, the CEO of WWF US earned over $1 million in compensation, with several staff members earning close to $500,000.[109] In 2021, the Nature Conservancy income was even higher, nearing $2 billion.[110] The CEO's salary is also well over $1 million.

It's exciting to see large sums of funding going to the environment sector overall – we have extreme challenges in the face of climate change – but it is important the wealth isn't concentrated into the hands of a few global organizations and their CEOs. Relying on these funds to trickle down is never going to be the best strategy forward. We need innovative ways of putting more funds into the hands of local people, who can do the hard graft of bringing communities together to advocate for the types of policies we want to see. A farmer who wants to continue using phosphates – a cause of climate change and environmental degradation – to protect their livelihood is unlikely to elect the types of politicians who will vote down the use of fossil-fuel based farming at the national level, where INGOs often try to influence. And an international agreement will do little to change the attitudes of the farmers and local people. If the local organizations are only seeing a smattering of funding from the money at the top, they will lack the resources to do what needs doing.

Closing civic space as a catalyst for change in the environment sector?

So what might change all this, if the environment sector is lacking the demand to change, unlike their development peers? Look no further than the reality of closing civic space, where environmental activists, in particular, have faced the most severe threats: harassment, detainment, and murder.[111] The environment provides fertile ground for populists to make a common enemy of those who want to protect the environment or human rights, and certainly those 'nasty' foreigners. Even in western countries, such as the UK, governments have accused environmental activists of getting in the way of 'ordinary people', imposing a growing set of laws against any form of protest. Environmental activists and the environmental movement are the enemy.

One of the key drivers of this attack on environmental actors, identified by the Funders' Initiative for Civil Society and Global

Greengrants, is the lack of solidarity between international and local organizations. Their strategies and approaches differ vastly, enabling governments and companies to divide and conquer on the ground. This is why XR attacks WWF: WWF tries to navigate a complex insider/outsider role with banks and other corporate entities and can therefore be perceived as 'the enemy' of actual change by the more fervent, front-line activists who see no role for such actors at all in a sustainable world.

Closing civic space would seem, therefore, to be a catalyst to recognize that we're all in this together. What do local civil societies and activists want and need from the environmental movement? In 2023, it's interesting to note that XR in the UK changed course, working actively with ENGOs as a way to bring more moderate voices into its fold. But how does this play out in other countries?

Changing the ENGO system to protect the environment

Our battles in the environmental movement are both hyper local and hyper international, and there is an opportunity to do far more building across the bridges of the different arms of the environmental movement. Michael Sutton, Executive Director of the Goldman Foundation (which awards the Goldman Environmental Prize), who has worked across the sector, sees huge potential: locally, activists need INGOs to connect their work across geographies, not just the financial resources they provide that don't currently make it to the ground, but also the access they provide to those in power. They can facilitate dialogue and influence where it's needed and bring local activists to the table.

Key questions for those working in the environmental sector include: is our model working to strengthen national approaches and connect with one another? Are there enough resources being shared between the international and local? Whose voices are heard on the international stage and how are ENGOs getting in the way of more voices being heard – or enabling this?

The human rights movement

The human rights movement that grew out of the Second World War has arguably suffered some of the most serious challenges to its existence, as the once widely accepted principles of human rights are coming under increasing attack – not just from authoritarian countries, but also from the original governments who were the front-line builders of the movement. In the UK, with the aftermath of Brexit, the government has threatened to withdraw from the European Convention on Human Rights, while in the US, states are increasingly attacking and removing hard-won freedoms around such things as reproductive rights, freedom of speech, and the right to protest.

The international human rights movement isn't as broad as either the environment or development sectors. Internationally, there are only two dominant players, Amnesty International and Human Rights Watch, though there are other important actors, including the International Federation for Human Rights (FIDH) and the Helsinki group, that shouldn't be excluded.

Arguably, the human rights movement is facing a more existential crisis: while the general causes of the humanitarian, development, and peacebuilding sectors are widely accepted as desirable (though subsets, like reproductive rights, remain contested), human rights are more politically charged. In spite of the Universal Declaration of Human Rights, the concept of human rights has, more recently, been framed not as universal, but instead as rooted in western foreign policy. The idea that human rights are for everyone hasn't resonated in non-democratic regimes, at least not in the way it was originally envisaged. Thus, human rights INGOs – and indeed other development organizations that take a rights-based approach – are effectively seen as political instruments of the west.

So when Amnesty decided to 'localize' and strengthen its brand at the national level, this became a red flag for more restrictive regimes, like those in India and Brazil, who used Amnesty's work as ammunition against all foreign INGOs, calling out 'foreign interference' and scapegoating them as being against security or, indeed, development, even if they were staffed by local citizens.[112]

Amnesty's localization efforts also raised concerns among local organizations who navigated the human rights space in different ways. Not only did this form of localizing potentially displace funding away from local organizations – there is some anecdotal evidence showing that rather than growing the space for human rights, it just displaced it – the clamp down on Amnesty's work led to a clamp down on all human rights actors, who were seen as guilty by association.

This raises an existential question for human rights INGOs: if localizing isn't the solution, what is the role of international civil society actors in this space?

The human rights INGO in modern times

While organizations like Amnesty and Human Rights Watch have been pivotal in raising attention to abuses of human rights, they started in a time when this work was scarce, and when the means of communications to bring things to the international stage did not exist as they do today. But do we still need an INGO, like Amnesty or Human Rights Watch, highlighting the wrongdoings of a government in China or Saudi Arabia?[113] Although internet restrictions are growing in some countries, there is a plethora of actors who are making issues known on the international stage, taking huge personal risks, and evading such restrictions through technologies like virtual private networks or VPNs. Furthermore, it could be argued that by strengthening these local actors and providing more resources, they may be better placed to hold their governments to account, and they can work in a way that's more sensitive to the local cultural environment.

'In essence, there's been a shift from an era when human rights were viewed as neutral in conflict and war situations – or the way certain governments treated their citizens. And to some degree that is no longer applicable in today's world', writes Rob Mudge. He cites academic Stephen Hopgood who argues that Amnesty is stuck in the past. 'That world has been overtaken by popular mobilization around a whole range of deeply problematic and complex issues, such as sex work or abortion ... Both sides will often claim human rights as part of their ideological or ethical position', says Hopgood.[114]

Working practices

Amnesty, for one, has also faced critiques about a toxic working environment, following the investigation into the death of an employee, Gaëtan Mootoo. The investigation found the root cause of Mootoo's death was an organizational culture within Amnesty that failed to look after staff.[115] Some of the harrowing issues that human rights organizations deal with – like torture and abuse – without commensurate support from the organization, can take a huge personal toll, making the need to look after staff critical. To be fair, this challenge isn't unique to human rights organizations: indeed, humanitarian workers routinely face the experience of going into a refugee camp or a war zone. However, humanitarian organizations have foundational support systems in place, like the work of the CHS (Core Humanitarian Standard) Alliance, among others. This type of support hasn't yet found its way into human rights organizations, perhaps in part because the sector is smaller and more siloed.

Human rights INGOs and solidarity

There are multiple initiatives that are looking at the future of the human rights movement, including the Symposium on Strength and Solidarity for Human Rights.[116] One thing they agree on – and that resonates with the findings of the RINGO Project across all sectors – is that the system needs to be steered from the ground, not the top. Embedding and building stronger respect for human rights in all societies is a local effort and one that requires solidarity. The human rights INGO needs to be in listening and co-creation mode to determine how best to serve those needs, rather than dictate them. Thus, asking questions, such as 'what do local human rights actors want and need from us?' and 'how can we facilitate that?', is better than dictating how they should implement human rights or calling their government to account. This means that in a country where civic space is closing, while it is important to call out the regime, INGOs should only do so if this is requested and underpinned by local actors. INGOs can facilitate dialogue, provide legal and other resources, and help local organizations to fundraise for their own needs. But imposing a big brand locally should only be done if local human rights actors agree it will enrich their space.

The traditional work of human rights INGOs – like advocacy on the international stage – is undoubtedly still needed, but arguably there's little point in doing so without the commensurate work on the ground. The world has changed since the Universal Declaration of Human Rights was first signed 70 years ago. Our methods, responses, and organizational design to uphold these also needs a radical overhaul, starting from a position of solidarity and humility.

The peacebuilding sector

In the world of INGOs, the peacebuilding sector is a relative newcomer. Peacebuilding movements are not new: International Peace Builders was founded in 1891 at an annual gathering of national peace societies from Europe and North America. Religious groups have been working on negotiating peace behind the scenes for years – like the Quaker intervention in the Biafran war in the late 1960s. And there was the anti-nuclear movement and growing global cohort of 'conscientious objectors'. But peacebuilding as a larger INGO sector only took off after the 1994 genocide in Rwanda. Prior to that, it didn't really have a name. 'Peacebuilding' was first mentioned by the UN in 1992, when Secretary General Boutros Boutros-Ghali launched the Agenda for Peace. This was at the end of the Cold War, when many political leaders and civil society activists were optimistically talking about a peace dividend and how to avoid confrontation in future.[117]

What happened in Rwanda, to many observers, was a 'preventable genocide'.[118] An INGO sector focusing on peace emerged out of the sentiment of 'never again' and quickly professionalized to cover the whole gamut of the conflict cycle: before, during, and after war, not just the work of 'peace and reconciliation', as became the main activity of humanitarian and development groups in post-conflict settings. International Alert, Search for Common Ground, Interpeace, and others all emerged during this tumultuous and reflective time.

Peacebuilding is effectively rooted in white saviourism. From the earliest days, prior to peacebuilding being professionalized, war has always been perceived as needing intervention by so-called 'neutral' forces outside of warring countries or regions: like the Camp David Accords, a peace deal between Israel and Egypt negotiated by American President Jimmy Carter; or the Dayton agreement, a peace agreement between Bosnia and Croatia overseen by French President Jacques Chirac and American President Bill Clinton. Heroic white men save the day!

'It's always been about the white man's burden', says Nikki de la Rosa, a former Country Director of International Alert in the Philippines, an organization that has now separated from International Alert to become an independent locally led organization, the Council for Climate and Conflict Action Asia.

'Because of this, the structures that were put in place were rooted in structural racism, a sense that we can't be trusted, that we don't have our own expertise'. Dylan Mathews, of Peace Direct, confirms this: 'for too long, there's an in-built assumption in the peacebuilding sector that local people can't be trusted, either with managing donor funds or in leading their own efforts without outside help'.

There are no clear external smoking guns in the sector – no mass scandals to drive change, no internal struggles that have hit the headlines – unlike in other INGO sectors. Nonetheless, there is a demand for change and structural racism is central to this demand. 'The whole business model of securing expert advice from HQ plays into this', says Nikki de la Rosa. She spoke about the fact that only the experts – say on gender, or mediation, or the private sector, were employed at headquarters (HQ), mainly represented by western-educated, western individuals. 'They assume they have the knowledge, and that local people have none'. She tells me that institutional racism is prevalent in International Alert. When the organization faced redundancies, people of colour were largely those who were let go – this was partly because they predominantly occupied operational roles in the organization, reflecting the fact that few senior leaders were people of colour.

Peace Direct, an organisation whose sole purpose is to support local actors in fragile countries, has led many discussions and reports on racism and decolonization in the sector, especially during the onset of the Black Lives Matter movement, when they recognized that the work they had been doing for 20 years hadn't made much traction. It was then that they posited that 'structural racism' is at the heart of why power hasn't shifted to local actors. It wasn't one or two organizations – it was endemic, as Dylan Mathews, their CEO explained to me.

The vast majority of issues that impact on humanitarian and development organizations impact the peacebuilding sector too. But one of the characteristics of the sector – the focus on external mediation – actually hardwires white saviourism into the operating model, rather than it just being an unspoken characteristic beneath the surface. 'There is a dominant sense that external mediation is preferable to locally led mediation. Local people are perceived as biased, and part of the conflict', says Mathews. 'So you have this whole industry that has been built up around this central perceived expertise, coupled with mistrust of local actors'.

Ironically, it's this bias that has arguably been at the forefront of enabling the sector to grow. Saferworld began as a research and advocacy organization, emerging out of the Cold War and the desire to end the use of nuclear weapons. But like other INGOs caught up in the expansion of international development, funded in part by growing aid budgets at the turn of the millennium, they expanded to offer more direct implementation and set up offices in the Middle East and North Africa in the early 2000s.

This growth in country offices, in turn, has led to the reinforcement of the white saviour bias, and undermines the confidence in local actors. When Peace Direct consulted their partners about this, they were told: 'if INGOs keep setting up offices, it means they have actually given up on us: they think we'll never be able to do this ourselves, that we'll never be at peace and will always need "mediators"'. For local peacebuilding actors, like Nikki de la Rosa, who have worked for years trying to build peace in their communities, this is not a pill they are prepared to swallow. 'Peace needs to come from the local community. We need to tell our own stories', she says. In the Council for Climate and Conflict Action Asia's parting letter to their colleagues in International Alert, they write:

> Thirteen years have passed since International Alert Philippines was conceived and established yet there seems to be no end in sight to the cycles of violent conflict in our country. The task is not finished, the vision has not been reached, and the mission continues to hold profound significance ... The formalization of our transition from an international to a local organization is a significant milestone in our journey towards achieving our vision of becoming independent, autonomous, and locally owned, embedding the legacy of our work within a fully locally-led peacebuilding organization.[119]

Peace doesn't happen overnight

Perhaps more than in other sectors, with the exception of human rights, one of the main critiques of the peacebuilding sector is that it has become 'projectized', as if through a year or a few years of focused work, peace can be achieved. But peace, of course, is a dynamic process, something that requires long-term investment and long-term processes to be embedded in any long-term cultural change. And for funders, whose models only award known outcomes, the peacebuilding model is obscure to measure. It's the only sector where the primary outcome is no outcome at all, and there is literally nothing to really sell to donors: 'you invested in country x, and look: nothing happened!'. As Dylan Mathews notes, 'it takes a leap of faith to believe that the investment was worthwhile. The concept of "improved social cohesion" is something academics have been grappling with for decades'. New ways of measuring success, led by local actors, not by donors, need to be normalized.

Finally, financial security is an issue for the international peacebuilding sector. Some – like International Alert – charge a direct fee (generally 12% indirect costs) to country offices to keep their HQ afloat. Unlike other brand name development organizations, who have massive public-facing fundraising arms, peacebuilding organizations rely almost entirely on institutional and philanthropic funding. As some funding leaders are looking to build and strengthen their own local funding models, the sources of funding for peacebuilding INGOs (and others) are increasingly threatened. Having built up their own top-heavy infrastructure, and now competing for funding with national civil society, INGOs may feel they have no choice but to extract what they can from country offices. But this time will no doubt come to an end, as organizations, like the former Philippine country office, secure their own independence.

And the rest

There are many other subsets of INGO sectors out there, many of which are actively exploring the issues of shifting power and localization. The sexual health and reproductive rights sector has done its own exploration through the TIME (Transforming INGO Models for Equity) initiative,[120] bringing together four INGOs working in sub-Saharan Africa. Their findings were not dissimilar to those of the RINGO Project: they found lack of trust between international and national partners, tokenism in engaging local people, unhealthy competition between international and national partners when INGOs open local offices, and excessive bureaucratic burdens from donors that are prejudiced against local actors. Their recommendations mirror those that have been discussed in this book, too.

Between the sectors: Negotiating solidarity and removing the silos

Civil society is necessarily messy. If we want freedom to organize and freedom to assemble, then we will always have differences in our approaches: religiously affiliated organizations may not always agree on reproductive or gender rights, for example. I'll make no comment on that here; however, it is worth discussing how progressive voices can navigate those differences in solidarity with local actors.

Humanitarian organizations, as noted earlier in this chapter, may water down human rights commitments to ensure long-term access in a country with more repressive governments. When this decision is taken, it should be done in collaboration with a range of civil society actors. Many local actors will be working across sectors: we certainly saw during the COVID-19 pandemic how local development organizations stepped in heroically to provide a range of humanitarian needs. They will be sensitive to local cultures but may still want to engage in solidarity. Considering positions on specific human rights issues or other areas of social justice need to be navigated and responses should be actively negotiated with progressive local civil society partners.

During a RINGO prototype in the Philippines, which looked at the intersection between climate justice and conflict, peacebuilding groups wanted to collaborate actively with the extractives sector, against the aims of some environmental organizations. Both had the aim of transitioning to a carbon-free future, but peacebuilding actors were acutely more sensitive to the potential consequence of a hard exit from coal on local actors in a community where conflict was endemic. As evident in this instance, the polarization of social and environmental justice issues, or the prioritization of one over the over, can lead to marginalization and resentment of one or more CSOs.

Lack of solidarity, especially among progressive civil society actors, can have radical, and often harmful, consequences for civil society overall. In countries where civic space has closed, it enables local governments to divide civil society. Solidarity is broken down rather than built up. In the end, all of civil society pays the price as governments restrict the efforts of everyone.

'Localization' or 'shifting power' away from INGOs may require more, rather than less, facilitation, either by international or local actors. As I have learned from the RINGO Project's systemic approach, there is really no such thing as a purely humanitarian, development, environmental, human rights, or peacebuilding organization. The issues we're tackling are multi-faceted, so our approach to organizing needs to be multifaceted too. Removing the silos is equally as important as paying attention to what happens within them as well.

There is an acute need to invest in the common infrastructure that can be shared among CSOs, partly as INGOs will shrink in size, and partly as a way to ensure that more collaboration, as opposed to competition, takes place. Ensuring funding for the spaces where civil society meets – common digital platforms and other spaces that keep local and national organizations connected and engaged – becomes more important in the new civil society landscape.

CHAPTER EIGHT
Renewal

In January 2024, a group of researchers launched a study with Partos, the membership association for Dutch INGOs, in which one of the surprising findings was that respondents in INGOs perceived that they had no power to change the system.[121] When presenting the findings in a global webinar, the virtual eye rollings were palpable. The findings from the Partos paper reflect the findings from a Humentum report on equitable development, which found that although INGOs were active in conversations about shifting power, there is far more talk than action. While 81% of respondents to an INGO survey reported aspiring to change their operating models, 'only 42% report implementing deliberate changes'.[122] Indeed, the RINGO Project's follow-up 2023 study 'Voices from the South: What Can INGOs and Funders do to Shift Power?' also found that although there is change, it continues to be painfully slow.[123]

The findings from Partos and other studies are unsurprising, however. When people perceive a long-standing intractable issue before them, and most levers for change are perceived as outside of their control, then the general response seems to be that there is nothing they can actually do to shift the system. So talking about the problem, rather than trying to change them, is the default and easier reaction.

There is no doubt that systems are hard to change. There are always levers outside of one person or one organization's control. But if a sufficient number of movers shift what *is* in their control – and work with others to influence what may be partly outside of their control – then it is entirely possible to achieve systems change. This is what happened with every significant systemic social change in history, from ending the slave trade in the 19th century, to universal suffrage in the early 20th century, to more recent movements that are succeeding in building a green economy[124] in many countries across the world.[125] I would argue that these were (and continue to be) far greater systemic challenges than changing the INGO sector and the aid system that supports it. In contrast, the changes being called for throughout this book should be entirely achievable within a short space of time.

An emerging cohort of INGOs and funders are working actively to try to shift power. HelpAge International, an organization that participated in the RINGO Project, has been supporting its country offices to achieve organizational independence, and has often looked at its work under the headline of 'stopping as success'.[126] Oxfam GB has agreed a strategy at its board level to 'decolonize' its practice. And in a recent article, Oxfam America uses its own organizational power to call out the flaws in USAID's own practices of localization, effectively lobbying against its own interest. The article points out that when international organizations establish independent, nationally registered organizations, these are treated as local entities by USAID. They are not local, says Oxfam America: '[w]hen an international entity registers nationally (as Oxfam has in Colombia) … it continues to draw on the tangible and intangible resources of its global counterparts – not simply funds but also networks, knowledge, infrastructure, skills, brand name, and other assets – giving it an unfair advantage over most local groups'.[127] Others, meanwhile, have already disrupted the system and designed an entirely different INGO model – like BRAC, the Bangladeshi-led INGO, now the largest INGO in the world and fully led from Bangladesh and without big restricted investments and control from western governments or philanthropy, surviving mainly on self-generated funds. Though BRAC, too, is also having a rethink of its role post-COVID[128] and of its relationships with local partners.

The reality is: INGOs and those who work with them do have the resources and the power to *shift the power*. But they need to overcome the fear: fear of loss, fear of failure, fear of exposure. They need to agree to be vulnerable and open to change, and recognize their own power and privilege. All of these fears are valid, but they're not the reason to maintain the status quo. Ultimately, however, not only will there be an ongoing role for INGOs (albeit smaller, more focused), it will be a pivotal role in helping to build a good society for all of us.

Telling a different story of success

The end of 2023 felt like a low point in internationalism, at least since the Second World War. The year was characterized by ever more conflict and failed political action around the climate crisis, and it was the hottest year on record, commensurate with increasing numbers of wildfires, floods, and storms. The war in Gaza left many of us looking at the futility of our efforts, as unprecedented civilian casualties increased, and a risk of famine is, at the time of writing, on the horizon. Meanwhile, the war in Ukraine has receded from the headlines, though it is still causing undue harm to countless numbers of innocent people, threatening to impact on the wider region too. In many corners of the world, there is an impression that things are getting worse, not better.

INGOs are not responsible for war. They are not responsible for climate change or inequality or failed diplomatic efforts. But their purpose, especially as part of their growing presence over the past half-century and more, was to contribute to the network of civic solutions to avoid or mitigate such calamities. Ironically, as their presence and resources grew, they moved further and further away from the solidaristic social movements that convened them at the outset.

This is not for lack of good intentions, but instead it is about the evolution of the institution itself and the story that enveloped so many INGOs from the beginning – one that bound the original rationale to its fate – that people in Africa or Asia or Latin America lacked capacity to solve their own problems, and that they were 'undeveloped'. Thus formed the structures that are now so ingrained in our international system, on which the more formal political institutions rely, and that the general public, at least in the west, look to when they see a failing system before their eyes.

The decolonization movement has grown in response to the realization that this system, far from saving the world, in reality, rewards only a small group of people, headquartered and resourced and deriving their power from the wealthier parts of the world. This small group of people has inadvertently replicated the inequality seen in wider society in our systems of civil society.

Worryingly, this has led to some people in the majority world looking away from civil society and democracy altogether. John Githongo, a journalist and activist in the anti-corruption movement, writes about the appeal of non-democratic models of governance in Africa, in particular. He finds that young people are looking more towards authoritarian states who are at least delivering decent livelihoods, reflecting on their own discontent about the lack of employment and the economy. He writes:

> This is not so much a contest against so-called western values of democracy and human rights but rather against what is understood, especially by youth and especially in the Global South, as western hypocrisy and double standards in the export of these values. The 'international community' of yesteryear meant an amorphous grouping of countries, NGOs, media organizations and other agencies decisively led by the USA and the EU, bolstered by key allies such as Australia, Canada and New Zealand. Not anymore.[129]

INGOs, by virtue of their models, have been implicated in failing to deliver the promises of democracy and freedom. Githongo calls for a new era of cooperation in civil society, strengthening local efforts at the same time as ensuring more equal relationships among international actors.

The rise of the decolonization movement has caught some in the international civil society sector off guard. 'We're not the enemy!' the more defensive in the sector will think. And, indeed, there are some fantastic people in the sector who are all motivated by the work of ending poverty, or saving the environment, or whatever just cause they're working on. But it can be difficult to hear the words 'go away', 'let go', or 'shift power'. Nonetheless, a call to action to shift power is a must. It won't do the job of ending climate change, or stopping wars, but it will create the building blocks we need to have more effective and empowered solutions in the long run, ones that are owned by the very people who are at the front lines of social change.

We need to start by telling ourselves a different story: that the role of international civil society actors isn't to solve all of our many global problems – it's to support and encourage and cajole people to bring about change in their societies, and to use their global connectivity to build influence on the international stage. As discussed in Chapter 2, our theory of change should be that a strong progressive civil society locally, with resources, power, voice, *and* international connections, will lead to better outcomes across all sectors and issues we are seeking to address: development, humanitarian, environment, and human rights alike.

To end this book on a positive note: in spite of the critiques of INGOs, and in spite of all of the institution's many flaws, there remains a need for some type of INGO for the future. In the course of the interviews that I conducted for this book, even the most vocal critics saw INGOs as a necessary part of the civil society mix. A 2021 study by the West Africa Civil Society Institute (WACSI) and RINGO found that 87% of over 600 respondents welcomed partnerships with international actors: INGOs and funders alike.[130]

'There are times when you need the INGOs as a buffer to protect yourself, especially in countries where civil society is at risk ... They can have partners, yet take the flack from the government. But they need to do this in a way that stands in solidarity with local civil society, and they don't need to do direct delivery', says Degan Ali, from Adeso, one of the first organizations to confront the power of INGOs head-on.

'I still see a role for INGOs, but it's not transferring money to local civil society organizations. I would rather see them working as advocacy partners, door openers ... the kind of political alliance that local civil society might need if they ask for it', says Viveka Carlestam, an international donor on the front lines of building the bilateral funding movement for localization.

How are we going to get there?

The RINGO Project is among many of the initiatives seeking to transform power and resourcing in civil society. Such initiatives proliferated during and after the COVID-19 pandemic, following the stark realization of the disparities between local and international actors when flying around the world was suddenly halted. RINGO offered a space for people, many of whom had been grappling with these issues for years, to reflect on why things haven't changed, and to imagine a different future. Some participants in the RINGO Project are going on to embed the prototypes[131] that were first launched in 2022, while other participants have developed their own initiatives in collaboration with each other.[132] RINGO's role has been to catalyse change in the systemic levers that no one actor can change alone, bringing together everyone in the system.

Others are convening INGOs to examine their own practice and build new models, including the Pledge for Change, the International Civil Society Centre's Power Shifters Lab, and the Partos Innovation Hub. New spaces are also emerging from outside northern actors, including the Network for Empowered Aid Response (NEAR) and the wider #ShiftThePower movement. The latter is convened by the Global Fund for Community Foundations, which has been central to building communities to innovate and transform civil society, from strengthening the demand for change among local actors, to offering new purpose and roles for international actors.[133]

None of these initiatives will transform the system on their own, but those participating in them are taking the first steps in doing so, and, most importantly, understand that they have the power to change things. If we can build more collaboration among the different actors, set some common goals, and take genuine steps towards them, change is around the corner.

Many working in INGOs or serving on their boards are asking: what is the blueprint for change? What is the new-model INGO? The problem is that this is the wrong question; knowing precisely 'what' needs to change still doesn't address the idea of 'how' one changes. How many reorganizations and new organizational strategies have we all witnessed happening every few years (some more frequently) with little impact on actual outcomes? Here's the bad news: there is no single blueprint for change.

However, although there is no blueprint for the INGO of the future, there is something that can help us: focusing on 'how' instead of 'what'. If I've learned anything in over 25 years in civil society, and certainly through working in collaboration with the #shiftthepower movement, it is that it's all about process: *how* we collaborate, *how* we work together, *how* we show up in this space. Building well thought-out, process-driven, equitable spaces for collaboration is the primary thing we need to engage with. Most sectors – and civil society isn't alone in this – are fixated on 'vision': what are we working towards, rather than how do we get there? Process becomes relegated to the back burner, and people revert to immediate issues and ongoing day-to-day churn. Some refer to this as the tyranny of the 'now': we want answers, we want solutions, but we're not prepared to dedicate the time to get there.

Investing in spaces, facilitation, and cross-collaboration (even among the many crises and emergencies and day-to-day challenges we all face in our respective spaces) and investing in the ability to listen, and to question our own personal motivations and power – these are, in my view, the most important actions that systems-changers need to take. *That* is the how. From good processes emerge actions and a willingness to shift what previously seemed intractable.

Going deeper

Some of the structural issues referred to in this book can't be addressed at the drop of a hat, nor through a simple tick-box exercise. They require all of us to go a bit deeper. The RINGO Project, and to an extent this book, while addressing systems change, has only started to touch on the matter of how we overcome structural challenges – structural racism, inclusion, diversity, and representation – in *a profound and transformative manner.* As Charles Kojo Van Dyck, from WACSI, says:

> Diversity is a complex issue interwoven with interconnected linkages, including race, geographical location, gender, age, social status, and generational differences. Addressing these elements requires a holistic understanding that extends beyond superficial changes in leadership. It calls for a meticulous examination of the structural foundations underpinning our organizations.

Anti-racism work, nonetheless, is being wilfully sidelined in organizations, argues Leena Bheeroo from Bond. It's easier to engage in a 'diversity, equity, and inclusion' exercise than the hard graft of cultural change involved in anti-racism work.[134]

Going deeper requires that we overcome fears and address genuine culture change. Indeed, fear was an oft-cited response about the barriers to change when I spoke to people about this book: fear of being accused of being 'racist', fear of being 'found out' – that the work they'd been doing for so long wasn't of value, or that they, too, were creaming off an inequitable system. But there were also other more immediate fears: fear of losing their jobs, with mortgages to pay and families to support, fear of being made redundant, both literally and figuratively. The life and career that people have defined for themselves may no longer be valid.

There is an innate tension between doing something meaningful that is deeper and less visible – that is, the hard stuff of addressing racism or patriarchy – versus making practical operational changes. You don't want any of this work to be sidelined into an easy-to-do tick-box exercise, but nor do you want it to sit solely in the realm of conversation, where it looks like work on shifting power now largely resides. After a while, those, too, become meaningless, unless they're turned into genuine action.

Those in the sector can make some changes to funding or risk processes, but genuine, long-term change has to peel back the layers of culture change, addressing our deeper fears about loss and purpose, and acknowledging the power and privilege that INGOs have had in civil society until now.

Accepting loss

Certainly, since the 1990s, INGOs, and, to a degree, philanthropy, have been wrapped in a bubble that embraces the idea that 'bigger is better'. As I've attempted to show throughout this book: not necessarily. As Michael Sutton of the Goldman Foundation says:

> I'm concerned about the future of the conservation movement; it's possible for groups to grow too big. When you do, what happens is that organizations lose their edge – they become so concerned with 'feeding the beast' that's all they can do. When they recruit executives nowadays, the only questions candidates get are how many people have you supervised, and how much money have you raised? Nothing about what you've accomplished or the actual mission at hand.

Jenny Hodgson of the Global Fund for Community Foundations says that we need to 'right-size a system that has been inequitable, and for INGOs, there needs to be a loss'.

Danny Sriskandarajah, the former head of Oxfam GB, has now gone onto head a think tank, the New Economics Foundation, whose founding premise is taken from the Schumacher school of thought, which is 'small is beautiful'.[135] German economist E.F Schumacher argued that people yearn for systems that are within their control: be it in organizations, politics, or economics. It applies firmly to the world of civil society. So many people working in and with larger international development organizations find themselves grappling with large-scale bureaucracy and not doing the real work they thought they signed up to do: working in solidarity with others to solve difficult social and environmental problems. Sometimes they find these organizations are at odds with their own personal values. Schumacher would argue that we need institutions that are human scale in which people can engage. Of course, the threats of artificial intelligence and the rise of corporate capitalism have taken this ambition further and further away from people's grasps, wherever in the world they operate. Can civil society counter these forces through a 'small is beautiful'-style ambition? I think so.

Some of the idea of 'loss' or 'smaller' is all down to perspective. As Sriskandarajah says:

> Oxfam GB gets more unrestricted [funds] in the UK than either Amnesty or Greenpeace. We think we're a poor development organization, but we're one of the richest advocacy organizations, with £100 million of net of unrestricted [funds]. We became rule takers, rather than recognizing that we can be one of the more powerful leaders in shifting power.

At the Shift the Power Summit in Bogota in December 2023, 700 people from all corners of the globe gathered, connecting smaller organizations from around the world to each other. They didn't feel 'small' in power, however. Sharing stories and connecting ideas and people created a bigger force for change – aka power – beyond each individual organization.

Although this can be a threat to the status quo for INGOs, it's one worth embracing. We can create an institutional model that is arguably better fit for purpose and that embodies equitable relationships, not just in words, but in funding, resources, and genuine relationships – and one that takes us back to our fundamental roots.

Hibak Kalfan, Executive Director of NEAR, a locally led network of humanitarian organizations across 34 countries, says that all of our institutions acknowledge the shared intention of the founding of INGOs like Oxfam, Save the Children, and CARE: 'they all started with an intention of helping their communities'. Now, she says,

'whether they are INGOs or NEAR network members, they share
the same intentions: how do we help our community; how do
we help the communities around us, and how do we go beyond
ourselves?'.[136]

The role of networks

Networks are more important than ever, and are one of the key
solutions in shifting power. INGOs still spend far too much time
replicating systems and competing for space with each other.
INGOs can achieve so much more through collaboration and
cooperation. This can come in the forms of building shared assets
and capacity: everything from investing in sharing back office
functions, to monitoring and evaluation mechanisms, like Talk To
Loop. There are many examples where common systems have made
things more efficient and effective in the INGO sphere: the Disasters
Emergency Committee in the UK, for example, ensures that at the
height of an emergency, communication with the general public is
streamlined and non-competitive. We also have huge opportunities
to share policy spaces more effectively, too. Does every INGO
need its own analysis to influence policy-makers with? Or can we
influence policy by investing in a small team, directly employed
by networks? Working on your specific issue doesn't have to mean
'brand' competition. We arguably need fewer and smaller INGOs
and more collaborative networks.

Networks have the power to not only streamline costs and
achieve focus; they also enforce collaboration and solidarity among
actors on shared agendas. They involve a different way of working
and thinking, and require humility, careful facilitation, and, most
importantly, giving up some control. If the task of shifting the system
is beyond the work of any individual or individual organization,
then it can only happen through collaborative efforts, best realized
through networks.

Networks are also important for us to do the interconnected work
of systems change. If we are going to transform the aid system or
the civil society ecosystem, this happens through bringing different
actors together, not through individual organizational action alone.

But one last word of caution: in the sector, membership-based
networks have often played to the lowest common denominator

of their members. Working through networks should increase our ambition to collectively act, not limit it.

Strengthening the demand

Degan Ali says that when she created the Pledge for Change, she wanted to create a community of INGO change agents. The risk, she acknowledges, is that whereas some INGOs decolonize, show up in solidarity, and shift power, others will continue to step in and dominate the space: they will accept the bulk of government or multilateral funding, impose their way of working, and fail to consult with and include local civil society on an equal footing.

'The best way to counter this threat in the INGO space is to strengthen the demand for change from local civil society: INGOs need local partners who understand the community; local partners can have power through demanding a more equal relationship with INGOs and the terms under which they'll accept working with them. Collectively, their power is greater than individually', says Ali.

The #ShiftThePower movement has articulated a manifesto to identify what it wants from international actors, on ways of what it calls 'deciding and doing'.[137] But we need more opportunities to create the mutual spaces where international actors, INGOs specifically, listen and learn from those behind it and co-create these new ways of working and organizing.

INGOs, however, can't lead this effort, as it would be anathema to the very concept of shifting power. All too often in this movement, even among progressive change agents, the dialogue is convened by northern actors, and is mostly populated and attended by those working with or in INGOs, speaking mainly about how to keep the institution alive, argues activist Themrise Khan. This, she suggests, is why she personally exited such discussions, as they were largely irrelevant. She suggests that these conversations should be asking: how do we end the neocolonial aid system? How do we show up in solidarity?[138]

Dylan Mathews heartily agrees: 'We have to rebalance the conversation. So much is happening in Europe or the US. We want majority world organizations to be demanding it: "this is our development, it's about what *we* want"'.

But thus far, INGOs are still staying in the safety of their own bubbles. Convenings led by those from the grassroots in the #ShiftThePower movement have seen little engagement from INGOs and international funders, as was evidenced by their stark absence at the Shift the Power Summit in Bogota at the end of 2023.

'When I attend online discussions led and convened by those whose experiences and contexts are similar to mine, the energy is different. Change seems possible. The issues are raw and real. We understand each other better so we are able to respond to each other better. This is the crux of change', says Themrise Khan.

Strengthening the demand side of the equation is critical. But INGOs need to show up and listen, not lead.

How does it all add up?

I never wanted to write a blueprint for change, as it would be anathema to the very premise of this book. Shifting power isn't about creating a checklist for change, or a singular model of organization. So much change is contextual, and everything about it needs to be rooted in participation from the allies you need to engage in that change agenda in the first place. Margit van Wessel, a Dutch academic, argues that if you start with the networks and organizations that are already trying to change the system, based on their own contextual understandings, you can transform not only the conversation, but the system.[139]

The deeper cultural change, arguably the real nub of this, will take time. But there are very tangible things that everyone in the system can do to accelerate that process.

First and foremost, INGOs can prioritize investment in local systems and local organizations: not by setting the explicit parameters and deciding beforehand what that investment might look like, but by genuinely investing. This means offering the obvious core funding to local organizations, but, in addition to that, supporting processes that increase genuine participation in decision-making, engagement, and feedback. That should impact on governance models and processes alike.

They can work to stop the direct implementation model that sees INGOs directly delivering programmes and services throughout the world. Where they do have local affiliates, if they haven't already done so, they should seek to nurture a more equitable model of partnership in confederations, where national chapters of INGOs have equal power in governance of the INGO at the very least, rather than being positioned as lesser 'country outposts'. These confederations, in turn, must also seek to be inclusive of allies in civil society at the local levels, helping to amplify the work of others, not drown them out.

Governance and strategic processes of INGOs can and should include genuinely local organizations, not solely the internationally affiliated branded chapter, either. They can and must include local communities in decision-making too. This can happen through new upward accountability models, some of which are described in Chapter 4, which involve communities in deciding the priorities of INGOs and in offering genuine proactive feedback and input in a continuous and ongoing cycle. New technologies make this ever more possible.

INGOs can use their power to share risks with donors, and not pass that risk onto local actors. Take the burden away from local civil society, don't pass it on. And it's not just financial risk: they can take the heat when civic space is closing and act in solidarity alongside the wishes of local civil society organizations, agreeing what that risk look like with others. INGOs can build and utilize new sets of metrics and practices that lead the way to show how they can be accountable to the communities where they're working and telling that story to donors.

INGOs should respond to community needs, not identify them from their own self-centred perspective. They can invest in processes to help communities identify what they want and need from INGOs, whether it's in the form of finance or non-financial support. They should focus on the assets that a community has first, not on what it lacks.

And INGOs should do less themselves and more through and with networks, letting go of power, brand, and control.

There is a difficult balancing act that INGOs need to play, one that's on face value full of contradictions: they need to use their power to shift power; they need to embrace modesty and humility to assert their role in the system; they need to use the muscle they do have to influence the wider aid system to also shift power.

Peace Direct refers to nine new roles for INGOs, many of which centre INGOs as advocates, connectors, and convenors, not as 'doers'.[140] The role is a smaller one, even, dare I say it, a beautiful one.

The end? Or the beginning?

I started this book by reflecting on my own observed experience working in and with INGOs. I fell out of love with an idea that my idealistic younger self had assumed when I first started working in the sector. But I still love civil society, in all its chaotic messiness: it's the one space outside of government or the private sector which I believe holds the primary seeds for building a better society. It has the potential to bring people together to co-create the world we want to see, not one that's imposed on us through rentier capitalism or increasingly undemocratic governments. But we need to harness that potential and build the institutions that will help make that potential a reality. And INGOs, I believe, can be useful institutions if they're prepared to do the hard work of transformation – of *renewal*.

Vu Le, a provocateur behind the blog Non-Profit AF says about civil society:

> I always say our sector is like air, whereas other sectors are like food. Air and food are both vital, but air does not get the same level of appreciation. Because it's invisible and automatically consumed, no one appreciates air until they are forced to pay attention, like when they're planning to dive underwater or climb a tall mountain, or when it's not there.[141]

This book has purposefully focused on the larger, international sector. However, it's certainly not all about them. 'It's big money that got us into this in the first place', says Nicola Banks, who established One World Together as a solidaristic model to focus more on building citizen power and an alternative system of funding rooted in the right values from the first place'.

Many will disagree with me when I say that we still need some form of INGO. Although we don't need the dominant INGOs of today, we continue to need a globally connected civil society. Institutional forms of a globally connected civil society, as opposed to the looser affiliations we see in social movements, can still be useful pillars of a good society. If we see INGOs as an institutional articulation of a collective voice that can act as a counterweight to the state or the private sector – one that can support people throughout civil societies and not dominate – then they are pivotal to our future. A re-imagined INGO may be just the thing we need.

FURTHER RESOURCES

Africa No Filter: https://africanofilter.org/
Bond: https://www.bond.org.uk
Deakin University Centre for Humanitarian Leadership:
https://centreforhumanitarianleadership.org
Decolonising Advisory Community: https://dacplatform.net
Humentum: https://humentum.org
International Civil Society Centre: https://icscentre.org
NEAR: https://www.near.ngo
Partos: https://www.partos.nl
Pledge for Change: https://pledgeforchange2030.org
#ShiftThePower movement: https://shiftthepower.org
The RINGO Project: https://rightscolab.org/ringo/

ACKNOWLEDGEMENTS

I appreciate this is a relatively short book, but there is a long list of people who I would like to thank who have contributed to its creation. I had no idea when I started what I was letting myself in for and you all helped smooth the bumps along the way.

First, I want to acknowledge the shared wisdom of the RINGO Project team: Nana Afadzinu, Charles Kojo Vandyck, Jimm Chick, Nancy Kankam Kusi, Janet Mawiyoo, Sparkle Richards, Jennie Richmond, David Winter, Akanimo Akpan, Rebecca Freeth, Lindsay Coates, Tara Rao, and Sarah Pugh. Back in late 2019, we had an idea about systems change in civil society that eventually became the RINGO Project. The team continues to support and inspire me on this journey, including indulging my desire to write 'RINGO, the book' in the first person and from my own perspective. Many of you read earlier chapters of the book and shaped its direction. This appreciation extends to colleagues at Rights CoLab, particularly Ed Rekosh, who believed in RINGO and offered me a home base from the start.

The RINGO Project participants and our allies in the #ShiftThePower movement have all embarked on their own journeys of change and disrupting the system, and I continue to follow them all with admiration. A standout thank you to Dr Nicola Banks and Dr Moses Isooba, who both patiently read a full manuscript and provided considerable feedback.

I want to thank the many people who took time out of their busy schedules to allow me to interview them for this book, sharing their personal stories and challenges. These individuals are referred to throughout the book, but a particular thank you goes to Degan Ali for her endless inspiration and mentorship in reminding me how to stay a true ally in this work.

To the people who helped me finalize and shape the book through research, editing and cover design – Sara Khaliq, Terese Jonsson, and Michelle Dwyer at Nice and Graphic in Peckham, alongside Stef Thelwell who peeked her head out of retirement and guided the cover design. And to my very good friend, writer and editor Bijal Vachharajani, who encouraged me to move beyond my 1,000-word blogging habit to finally write a whole damn book.

I certainly need to extend a debt of gratitude to the team at Practical Action Publishing, particularly Jutta Mackwell and Chloe Callan-Foster, who stepped in and saved my bacon at the very last minute with their belief in this project.

I could not have completed the book without a grant from the Robert Bosch Foundation, which generously allowed me to take the space to write, something that is rare these days. Miriam Brandner and Patrick Steiner-Hirth, in particular, have recognized the power of stronger local civil societies and sought to invest in the hard work of systems change.

To my old teachers and friends from the LSE cohort of 1996–97, in particular James Putzel, Paolo de Renzio, and Francisco 'Pancho' Lara: thank you for challenging me intellectually, and for letting me use your stories … and for being there for over 25 years from when I first started learning about the good, the bad, and the ugly of 'international development'.

Lastly, to my husband Jon Magidsohn, for his endless patience and support (and for always having to point out my extreme over-use of hyphens and commas, a lesson which I never seem to learn).

ENDNOTES

Introduction

[1] See, for example, USAID, 'Donor Statement on Supporting Locally Led Development', 13 December, 2022, https://www.usaid.gov/localization/donor-statement-on-supporting-locally-led-development; Ann Danaiya Usher, 'Sweden Opens NGO Funding Pool to Global Competition, Terminates All Contracts with Swedish Actors', Development Today, 21 March, 2024, https://development-today.com/archive/2024/dt-3--2024/sidas-ngo-aid-no-longer-restricted-to-swedish-organisations.-civil-society-funding-to-be-untied.
[2] RINGO Project, 'The RINGO Project: Re-imagining the INGO and the Role of Global Civil Society', RightsCoLab, 2024, https://rightscolab.org/ringo; #ShiftThePower, 'Another Way is Possible', 2023, https://shiftthepower.org.

Chapter 1

[3] John Eriksson and contributors, *The International Response to Conflict and Genocide: Lessons from the Rwanda Experience: Synthesis Report*, ODI, March, 1996, https://www.oecd.org/derec/50189495.pdf.
[4] Edelman, 'Edelman Trust Barometer 2023', 28 November, 2022, https://www.edelman.com/sites/g/files/aatuss191/files/2023-03/2023%20Edelman%20Trust%20Barometer%20Global%20Report%20FINAL.pdf.
[5] Philip Gourevitch, 'Alms Dealers; Can You Provide Humanitarian Aid Without Facilitating Conflicts?', *The New Yorker,* 4 October, 2010, https://www.newyorker.com/magazine/2010/10/11/alms-dealers.

[6] Lucy Rodgers, 'Haiti Quake: Why isn't Aid Money Going to Haitians?', BBC News, 12 January, 2013, https://www.bbc.co.uk/news/world-latin-america-20949624.

[7] Angela Dewan, Bharati Naik, and Joshua Berlinger, 'Oxfam's Deputy CEO Resigns Over Sex Crimes Scandal', CNN World, 12 February, 2018, https://edition.cnn.com/2018/02/12/europe/oxfam-scandal-intl/index.html.

[8] Barney Tallack, 'Transform or Die? Existential Questions and Ways Forward for INGOs', Bond, 6 July, 2020, https://www.bond.org.uk/news/2020/07/transform-or-die-existential-questions-and-ways-forward-for-ingos/.

[9] Eleanor Davey, John Borton, and Matthew Foley, 'A History of the Humanitarian System: Western Origins and Foundations', Humanitarian Policy Group Working Paper, ODI, 18 June, 2013, https://odi.org/en/publications/a-history-of-the-humanitarian-system-western-origins-and-foundations/.

[10] Andrew Purkis, 'Charities, Knitting and Democracy', *The Guardian*, 4 September, 2014, https://www.theguardian.com/society/2014/sep/04/charities-knitting-democracy-brooks-newmark.

[11] Parliament UK, 'Third-World Debt', Parliament UK Publications and Records, 22 June, 2004, https://publications.parliament.uk/pa/cm200304/cmhansrd/vo040622/text/40622w03.htm.

[12] Directorate General for Maritime Affairs and Fisheries, 'An Historic Achievement: Treaty of the High Seas is Adopted', European Commission, 19 June, 2023, https://oceans-and-fisheries.ec.europa.eu/news/historic-achievement-treaty-high-seas-adopted-2023-06-19_en.

[13] Francis Fukuyama, *The End of History and the Last Man*, Harmondsworth: Penguin, 1992.

[14] Seattle.Gov, 'World Trade Organization Protests in Seattle', Seattle Municipal Archives, August, 2023, https://www.seattle.gov/cityarchives/exhibits-and-education/digital-document-libraries/world-trade-organization-protests-in-seattle.

[15] See, for example, Civicus, 'Monitor Tracking Civic Space', 2024, https://monitor.civicus.org.

[16] Jenny Hodgson, 'The Birth of #ShiftThePower', The Global Fund for Community Foundations, 7 September, 2021, https://globalfundcommunityfoundations.org/blog/the-birth-of-shiftthepower.

[17] RINGO Project, 'The RINGO Project: Re-imagining the INGO and the Role of Global Civil Society', RightsCoLab, 2024, https://rightscolab.org/ringo; #ShiftThePower, 'Another Way is Possible', 2023, https://shiftthepower.org.

[18] Peter Walton (former CEO, Australian Red Cross), email message to the author, 5 February, 2024.

Chapter 2

[19] National Network of Local Philanthropy Development in Ukraine, 'If Not Now, When?', 2022, https://philanthropy.com.ua/en/program/view/akso-ne-zaraz-koli.

[20] Disasters Emergency Committee, 'The Appeal', Ukraine Humanitarian Appeal Six Month Report, 30 January, 2023.

[21] #ShiftThePower, 'An Open Letter to International NGOs Who Are Looking to "Localise" Their Operations', openDemocracy, 8 March, 2020, https://www.opendemocracy.net/en/transformation/an-open-letter-to-international-ngos-who-are-looking-to-localise-their-operations/.

[22] Ringo Project, 'Fostering Equitable North-South Civil Society Partnerships: Voices From the South', RightsCoLab, March, 2021, https://rightscolab.org/ringo-projects-first-research-report-voices-from-the-south/.

[23] Stowarzyszenie Interwencji Prawnej, 'Open Letter to International Organisations and Donors', 3 November, 2022, https://interwencjaprawna.pl/en/open-letter-to-international-organisations-and-donors/.

[24] Abigail R. Hall Blanco, 'Nearly 60 Years After the War on Poverty, Why is Appalachia Still Struggling?', Bellarmine University, 2021.

[25] Themrise Khan, Kanakulya Dickson, and Maika Sondarjee, eds. *White Saviourism in International Development: Theories, Practices and Lived Experiences*, Wakefield, Québec: Daraja Press, 2023.

[26] Marie-Rose Romain Murphy, 'Is the Aid Sector Tèt Anba?', CDA Collaborative, June, 2023, https://www.cdacollaborative.org/blog/is-the-aid-sector-tet-anba/.

Chapter 3

[27] TNN, 'Foreign-Funded NGOs Stalling Development: IB Report', Times of India, 12 June, 2014, https://timesofindia.indiatimes.com/india/foreign-funded-ngos-stalling-development-ib-report/articleshow/36411169.cms; Dhanya Rajendran, 'The Intelligence Bureau Report On NGOs And What It Says, The News Minute, 25 February, 2015, https://www.thenewsminute.com/news/intelligence-bureau-report-ngos-and-what-it-says-21256.

[28] Express News Service, 'Home Ministry Cancels Registration of Five NGOs for "violation" of FCRA', The Indian Express, 4 April, 2024, https://indianexpress.com/article/india/home-ministry-cancels-registration-of-five-ngos-for-violation-of-fcra-9250053/.

[29] See, for example, Julian Oram and Deborah Doane, 'Why Shrinking Civil Society Space Matters in International Development and Humanitarian Actions', European Foundation Centre and the Funders Initiative for Civil Society, 2017, https://efc.issuelab.org/resources/29212/29212.pdf.

[30] Andrew Purkis, 'Charities, Knitting and Democracy', The Guardian, 4 September, 2014, https://www.theguardian.com/society/2014/sep/04/charities-knitting-democracy-brooks-newmark.

[31] Sarah Pugh and Deborah Doane, 'Solidarity in Times of Scrutiny', International Civil Society Centre, October, 2019. https://icscentre.org/2020/06/09/solidarity-in-times-of-scrutiny-key-learnings-for-civil-society-coalitions/

[32] Save the Children, Holding Ourselves to Account in 2021, 2023, https://resourcecentre.savethechildren.net/document/save-the-children-global-accountability-report-2021-holding-ourselves-to-account-in-2021/.

[33] Alex Cole-Hamilton, 'Why INGOs Need to Put Power Analysis at the Heart of Governance', Bond, 15 December, 2020, https://www.bond.org.uk/news/2020/12/why-ingos-need-to-put-power-analysis-at-the-heart-of-governance/.

[34] Marilyn Scholl and Arthur Sherwood, 'Four Pillars of Cooperative Governance', Columinate, 4 January, 2014, https://columinate.coop/four-pillars-of-cooperative-governance-cg/.

[35] MSF, Governance in MSF International Structure, Entities and Platforms, 2021, https://www.msf.org/sites/default/files/2022-09/assohistory/2021%20MSF%20Governance.pdf.

[36] Tim Boyes-Watson, 'Towards a Theory of Transformation of the INGO Operating Model', Fair Funding Solutions, 27 July, 2023, https://fairfunding.solutions/2023/07/27/towards-a-theory-of-transformation-of-the-ingo-operating-model/.

[1a] Amy Paul, Craig Jolley, and Aubra Anthony, Reflecting the Past, Shaping the Future: Making AI Work for International Development, USAID, 2023, https://www.usaid.gov/sites/default/files/2022-05/AI-ML-in-Development.pdf.

[1b] Mustafa Suleyman and Michael Bhaskar, The Coming Wave: Technology, Power and the 21st Century's Greatest Dilemma, London: Bodley Head, 2023.

Chapter 4

[37] Mia Roesdahl, 'Chain of Influence Framework for Systems Change – Shifting Power to Local Actors', Conducive Space for Peace, March, 2022, https://www.conducivespace.org/2022/05/24/chain-of-influence-framework-for-systems-change-shifting-power-to-local-actors/.

[38] Karolina Soliar (National Network of Local Philanthropy, Ukraine), email message to the author, 4 February, 2024.

[39] Daniel Martin, 'Britain Will Send £1.3 Billion in Aid to Countries that Won't Join Us in Condemning Vladimir Putin's Invasion of Ukraine', *Daily Mail*, 1 April, 2022, https://www.dailymail.co.uk/news/article-10674583/Britain-send-1-3billion-aid-countries-wont-join-condemning-Vladimir-Putin.html.

[40] Ben Hayes and Poonam Joshi, 'Rethinking Civic Space in an Age of Intersectional Crises: A Briefing for Funders' Initiative for Civil Society at Global Dialogue, May, 2020, https://global-dialogue.org/rethinking-civic-space/.

[41] Carelle Mang-Benza, 'An Alternative to Direction & Control? Response to the Draft CRA Guidance on Grants to Non-Qualified Donees', Cooperation Canada, 23 February, 2023, https://cooperation.ca/an-alternative-to-direction-control/.

[42] Independent Commission for Aid Impact, 'Tackling Fraud in UK Aid: A Rapid Review', April, 2021, https://icai.independent.gov.uk/html-version/tackling-fraud-in-uk-aid/.

[43] Christian Aid, 'Call for Partnership Application Form', 10 January, 2023, https://www.christianaid.org.uk/resources/our-work/call-partnership-application-form.

[44] Lindsey Hamsik, 'Managing Risk in International Aid And Local NGO Partnerships', InterAction, 6 March, 2019, https://www.interaction.org/blog/managing-risk-in-international-and-local-ngo-partnerships/.

[45] . Michael Vincent Mercado, 'Amidst the Limitations of Traditional Aid, Beacons of Hope Emerge', Global Fund for Community Foundations, 12 July, 2023, https://globalfundcommunityfoundations.org/blog/amidst-the-limitations-of-traditional-aid-beacons-of-hope-emerge/.

[46] Marie-Rose Romain Murphy, 'Is The Aid Sector Tèt Anba?', CDA Collaborative, June, 2023, https://www.cdacollaborative.org/blog/is-the-aid-sector-tet-anba/.

[47] Sadaf Shallwani and Shama Dossa, 'Evaluation and the White Gaze in International Development', in *White Saviourism in International Development: Theories, Practices and Lived Experiences*,

eds. Themrise Khan, Kanakulya Dickson, and Maika Sondarjee (Wakefield, Québec: Daraja Press, 2023), p. 43.
[48] Participant, at 'Decolonising Aid: Perspectives from Civil Society in Francophone Sub-Saharan Africa', West Africa Civil Society Institute webinar, 2 August, 2023.
[49] Isabella Jean, at RINGO Learning Festival, November, 2022.

Chapter 5

[50] Peace Direct, 'Transforming Partnerships in International Cooperation', August, 2023, https://www.peacedirect.org/transforming-partnerships/.
[51] Avis William, 'Funding Mechanisms to Local CSOs', K4D Helpdesk Report No.1136, Institute of Development Studies, 6 May, 2022, https://www.ids.ac.uk/publications/funding-mechanisms-to-local-csos/.
[52] USAID, 'Donor Statement on Supporting Locally Led Development', 13 December, 2022, https://www.usaid.gov/localization/donor-statement-on-supporting-locally-led-development.
[53] Peace Direct, 'Time to Decolonise Aid', 2021, https://www.peacedirect.org/time-to-decolonise-aid/.
[54] Charity So White, 'Defining Racism', Runnymede Trust, September, 2017, https://charitysowhite.org/defining-racism.
[55] Rebecca Freeth, Akanimo Akpan, and Mahmood Sonday, 'Dismantling Structural Racism in Organisational Systems', *Journal of Awareness-Based Systems Change*, 3(2), pp. 175–195, 2023, https://jabsc.org/index.php/jabsc/article/view/6282/5773.
[56] West Africa Civil Society Institute, 'Fostering Equitable North–South Civil Society Partnerships: Voices From The South', March, 2021, https://wacsi.org/fostering-equitable-north-south-civil-society-partnerships-voices-from-the-south/; RINGO Project, 'Inquiry Process Synthesis Report', RightsCoLab, September, 2021, https://rightscolab.org/inquiry-process-synthesis-report/.
[57] Themrise Khan, Kanakulya Dickson, and Maika Sondarjee, eds. *White Saviourism in International Development: Theories, Practices and Lived Experiences*, Wakefield, Québec: Daraja Press, 2023.
[58] OECD, 'Civil Society Engagement in Development Co-operation', OECD Development Co-operation Directorate, 2021, https://www.oecd.org/dac/civil-society-engagement-in-development-co-operation.htm.
[59] OECD, 'Untied Aid', 2023, https://www.oecd.org/dac/financing-sustainable-development/development-finance-standards/untied-aid.htm.

60 USAID, 'Localization at USAID: The Vision and Approach', August, 2022, https://www.usaid.gov/sites/default/files/2022-12/USAIDs_Localization_Vision-508.pdf.

61 Viveka Carlsam (SIDA), interview with author, August, 2023; see also Fran Girling-Morris, 'Donor Approaches to Overheads for Local and International Partners', Development Initiatives and UNICEF, February, 2023, https://devinit.org/resources/donor-approaches-overheads-local-national-partners/.

62 Courtenay Cabot Venton, *Passing the Buck: The Economics of Localising International Assistance*, The Sharetrust, November, 2022, https://thesharetrust.org/resources/2022/11/14/passing-the-buck-the-economics-of-localizing-international-assistance.

63 International Monetary Fund, 'Government Expenditure, Percent of GDP', 2021, https://www.imf.org/external/datamapper/profile/BFA; MINECOFIN, 'Government Outlines Spending Priorities for 2023-24', 3 May, 2023, https://www.parliament.gov.rw/news-detail?tx_news_pi1%5Baction%5D=detail&tx_news_pi1%5Bcontroller%5D=News&tx_news_pi1%5Bnews%5D=29337&cHash=4d878df648ff83f2e98ce92f60f3700b#:~:text=Key%20priorities%20for%20the%202023,and%20support%20to%20micro%2C%20small%2C.

64 Gavi, 'The Bill & Melinda Gates Foundation', 29 July, 2020, https://www.gavi.org/investing-gavi/funding/donor-profiles/bill-melinda-gates-foundation.

65 Julia Belluz, 'The Media Loves the Gates Foundation. These Experts are More Skeptical.' *Vox*, 10 June, 2015, https://www.vox.com/2015/6/10/8760199/gates-foundation-criticism.

66 Andreas Fuchs and Hannes Öhler, 'Does Private Aid Follow the Flag? An Empirical Analysis of Humanitarian Assistance', *The World Economy*, 44(3), pp. 671–705, 2020, https://onlinelibrary.wiley.com/doi/full/10.1111/twec.13021.

67 Edgar Villanueva, *Decolonizing Wealth: Indigenous Wisdom to Heal Divides and Restore Balance*, Oakland, California: Berrett-Koehler Publishers, 2018.

68 Open Society Foundations, 'Soros and Open Society Foundations Give $100 Million to Human Rights Watch', 6 September, 2010, https://www.opensocietyfoundations.org/newsroom/soros-and-open-society-foundations-give-100-million-human-rights-watch; WWF, 'WWF Receives $100 Million for Nature-Based Climate Solutions from the Bezos Earth Fund', 16 November, 2020, https://www.worldwildlife.org/press-releases/wwf-receives-100-million-for-nature-based-climate-solutions-from-the-bezos-earth-fund.

69 Avantika Chilkoti, 'The Super-Rich are Trying New Approaches

to Philanthropy', *The Economist*, 10 January, 2024, https://www.economist.com/special-report/2024/01/10/the-super-rich-are-trying-new-approaches-to-philanthropy.

[70] Lankelly Chase, 'Lankelly Chase to Wholly Redistribute its Assets Over the Next Five Years', 2023, https://lankellychase.org.uk/news/lankelly-chase-to-wholly-redistribute-its-assessts-over-the-next-five-years/.

[71] Plan International, *Worldwide Annual Review 2022*, 30 June, 2022, https://plan-international.org/uploads/2023/01/AnnualReview2022-EN-2.pdf.

[72] Plan International, *Worldwide Annual Reviews 2010–2022*, 2022, https://plan-international.org/publications/plan-international-worldwide-annual-reviews-2010-2022/.

[73] Save the Children International, *Trustees' Report, Strategic Report and Financial Statements for 2022*, December, 2022, https://resourcecentre.savethechildren.net/pdf/SCI-Trustees-Report-and-Financial-Statements-2022.pdf.

[74] Letter to Ani Dasgupta, President and CEO, World Resources Institute, 15 November, 2023, signed by 42 organizations, including the RINGO Project.

[75] Nicola Banks and Dan Brockington, 'Growth and Change in Britain's Development NGO Sector', *Development in Practice*, 30(6), pp. 706–721, 2020, https://www.tandfonline.com/doi/full/10.1080/09614524.2020.1801587.

[76] Danny Sriskandarajah, interview with author, 17 August, 2023.

[77] Humentum, 'New Findings Show How Funders Need to Break NGO Starvation Cycle', 28 March, 2022, https://humentum.org/blog-media/new-findings-show-how-funders-need-to-break-the-ngo-starvation-cycle/.

[78] Susannah Pickering-Saqqa, 'How Reliant are Big Development NGOs on UK Aid Money?', The Conversation, 16 February, 2018, https://theconversation.com/how-reliant-are-big-development-ngos-on-uk-aid-money-91708.

[79] Alex Tilley, 'A New Frontier in Aid Transparency? Private Sector Aid Contractors', Publish What You Fund, 23 September, 2023, https://www.publishwhatyoufund.org/2023/09/a-new-frontier-in-aid-transparency-private-sector-aid-contractors/.

[80] Alex Tilley, 'A New Frontier in Aid Transparency? Private Sector Aid Contractors', Publish What You Fund, 23 September, 2023, https://www.publishwhatyoufund.org/2023/09/a-new-frontier-in-aid-transparency-private-sector-aid-contractors/.

[81] Justin Sandefur, 'USAID Localization by the Numbers', Center for Global Development, 17 November, 2022, https://cgdev.org/blog/usaid-localization-numbers.

[82] The Equity Index, 'Who We Are', 2024, https://theequityindex. org/#:~:text=We%20are%20an%20anti%2Dracist,see%20the%20 Our%20Projects%20tab.
[83] Joanne Bauer, 'Making Rights Material', RightsCoLab, 23 April, 2021, https://rightscolab.org/making-rights-material/.
[84]Zambian Governance Foundation, 'Our Initiatives', 2024, https:// www.zgf.org.zm/our-initiatives/.

Chapter 6

[85] Bond, *Taking British Politics and Colonialism Out of Our Language: Bond's Language Guide*, 2021, https://www.bond.org.uk/wp-content/uploads/2021/05/Bond_Decoloinising-and-depoliticising_updated-2022.pdf.
Heinz Greijin, Gervin Chanase, Alan Fowler, et al. *Dream Paper: Shift the Power*, Partos, January, 2022, https://www.partos.nl/wp-content/uploads/2022/01/Partos-Dreampaper-Shift-the-Power-v5.pdf.
[86] Hilary Footit, Angela Crack, and Wine Tesseur, *Respecting Communities in International Development: Languages and Cultural Understanding*, intrac, June, 2018, https://www.intrac.org/wpcms/wp-content/uploads/2018/06/Listening_zones_report_-EN.pdf.
[87] RightsCoLab, 'VIDEO – Ringo Community Gathering: Language', June, 2023, https://rightscolab.org/video-ringo-community-gathering-language-june-2023/.
[88] Lerato Mogoatlhe, *Why Change the Way We Write About Africa? A Storyteller's Guide to Reframing Africa*, Africa No Filter, February, 2022, https://africanofilter.org/documents/Why_Change_The_Way_We_Write_About_Africa.pdf.
[89] Rose Caldwell, 'Authentic Storytelling is Now a Priority for Us', International Broadcasting Trust, 25 April, 2023, https://ibt.org.uk/blog/authentic-storytelling-is-now-a-priority-for-us/.
[90] Enrique Mendizabal, 'Local Research for Local Problems – Who Gets the Money?' On Think Tanks, 8 August, 2023, https://onthinktanks.org/articles/local-research-for-local-problems-who-gets-the-money/.
[91] Enrique Mendizabal, 'Local Research for Local Problems – Who Gets the Money?' On Think Tanks, 8 August, 2023, https://onthinktanks.org/articles/local-research-for-local-problems-who-gets-the-money/.
[92] Robert Chambers, *Rural Development: Putting the Last First*, 2nd ed, Oxon: Routledge, 2013; Robert Chambers, *Whose Reality Counts? Putting the First Last*, Rugby: Practical Action Publishing, 1997.

[93] Tosca Bruno-Van Vijfeijken, 'Onward with Reimagining INGO Models: Charles Kojo Vandyck @ RINGO/WACSI', *NGO Soul + Strategy*, podcast, 22 February, 2024, https://www.buzzsprout.com/708738/14556703-071-onward-with-reimagining-ingo-models-charles-kojo-vandyck-ringo-wacsi.

[94] Eleanor Davey, John Borton, and Matthew Foley, 'A History of the Humanitarian System Western Origins and Foundations', Humanitarian Policy Group Working Paper, ODI, June, 2013, https://odi.org/en/publications/a-history-of-the-humanitarian-system-western-origins-and-foundations/.

[95] International Development Research Centre, 'How 10 Years of Support has Made African Think Tanks Stronger', 3 October, 2019, https://idrc-crdi.ca/en/research-in-action/how-10-years-support-has-made-african-think-tanks-stronger.

[96] Talk To Loop, 'Community Feedback Made Easy', 2024, https://talktoloop.org/.

[97] RightsCoLab, 'Voices from the South: What can INGOs and Funders do to Shift Power?', March, 2024, https://rightscolab.org/ringo-projects-first-research-report-voices-from-the-south/.

Chapter 7

[98] Sabelo J. Ndlovu-Gatsheni, 'Rethinking Development in the Age of Global Coloniality', in *Rethinking and Unthinking Development: Perspectives on Inequality and Poverty in South Africa and Zimbabwe*, eds. Busani Mpofu and Sabelo J. Ndlovu-Gatsheni (Oxford: Berghahn Books, 2019), pp. 27–49.

[99] Ashley Betteridge, 'Why Indonesia is Right to Limit NGOs Post-Disaster', Devpolicyblog, 18 October, 2018, https://devpolicy.org/why-indonesia-is-right-to-limit-ngos-post-disaster-20181018/.

[100] Navi Pillay, John H. Knox, and Kathy MacKinnon, *Embedding Human Rights in Nature Conservation: From Intent to Action*, WWF, 17 November, 2020, https://wwfasia.awsassets.panda.org/downloads/independent_panel_report__embedding_human_rights_in_conservation.pdf.

[101] Matthew Taylor, 'Cop26 will be Whitest and Most Privileged Ever, Warn Campaigners', *The Guardian*, 30 October, 2021, https://www.theguardian.com/environment/2021/oct/30/cop26-will-be-whitest-and-most-privileged-ever-warn-campaigners.

[102] Greenpeace International, *Working with Indigenous People: Policy on Indigenous Rights*, January, 2017, https://www.greenpeace.org/static/planet4-international-stateless/2021/04/d87e4f72-policy-on-indigenous-rights.pdf.

103 Jon Ungoed-Thomas, 'WWF Shelved Report Exposing River Wye Pollution "to Keep Tesco Happy", *The Guardian,* 2 March, 2024, https://www.theguardian.com/environment/2024/mar/02/wwf-shelved-report-exposing-river-wye-pollution-to-keep-tesco-happy.

104 Damien Gayle, 'Environment Charities Lag Behind Other UK Sectors in Racial Diversity, Study Finds', *The Guardian*, 7 February, 2024, https://www.theguardian.com/environment/2024/feb/07/environment-charities-lag-behind-other-uk-sectors-in-racial-diversity-study-finds#:~:text=Only%20about%20one%20in%2020,of%20organisations%2C%20the%20research%20found.

105 Kara Kia, 'Greta Thunberg, David Attenborough and Environmentalism's White Saviour Problem', Popsugar, 18 November, 2020, https://www.popsugar.co.uk/news/environmentalism-white-saviour-complex-essay-47973371.

106 Conservation International, 'Board of Directors', 2024, https://www.conservation.org/about/board-of-directors.

107 Elizabeth Day, 'Trudie Styler: Why I Had To Use My Celebrity To Try To Save the Rainforest', *The Observer,* 22 March, 2009, https://www.theguardian.com/environment/2009/mar/22/trudie-styler-environmentalist.

108 WWF, *Annual Review*, 2020, https://wwfint.awsassets.panda.org/downloads/wwfintl_annualreview2020.pdf.

109 WWF, 'Form 990: Return of Organization Exempt From Income Tax', 2020, https://files.worldwildlife.org/wwfcmsprod/files/FinancialReport/file/37eyvkvty_WORLD_WILDLIFE_FUND_990_2019_Public.pdf?_ga=2.20555960.1607555337.1712823213-1881677271.1712823213.

110 The Nature Conservancy, *TNC 2022 Global Annual Report*, 2022, https://www.nature.org/en-us/about-us/who-we-are/accountability/annual-report/2022-annual-report/.

111 Global Witness, 'Our Inspiration: Names of Those Murdered in 2022', 15 September, 2023, https://www.globalwitness.org/en/campaigns/environmental-activists/standing-firm/.

112 TNN, 'Foreign-Funded NGOs Stalling Development: IB Report', *Times of India*, 12 June, 2014, https://timesofindia.indiatimes.com/india/foreign-funded-ngos-stalling-development-ib-report/articleshow/36411169.cms; Dhanya Rajendran, 'The Intelligence Bureau Report On NGOs And What It Says, *The News Minute*, 25 February, 2015, https://www.thenewsminute.com/news/intelligence-bureau-report-ngos-and-what-it-says-21256.

113 Rob Mudge, 'Amnesty International: The Good, the Bad and the Ugly?', *DW*, 28 May, 2021, https://www.dw.com/en/amnesty-international-the-good-the-bad-and-the-ugly/a-57680902.

114 Rob Mudge, 'Amnesty International: The Good, the Bad and the Ugly?', *DW*, 28 May, 2021, https://www.dw.com/en/amnesty-international-the-good-the-bad-and-the-ugly/a-57680902.

115 The Konterra Group, *Amnesty International: Staff Wellbeing Review*, January, 2019, https://www.amnesty.org/en/wp-content/uploads/2021/05/ORG6097632019ENGLISH.pdf.

116 Akwe Amosu and Peter Coccoma, '32. South Africa: The Challenge of Offering Solidarity Without Strings', *Strength and Solidarity*, podcast, 29 March, 2023, https://strengthandsolidarity.org/podcast/32-south-africa-the-challenge-of-offering-solidarity-without-strings/. and https://strengthandsolidarity.org

117 Boutros Boutros-Ghali, *An Agenda for Peace: Preventative Diplomacy, Peacemaking and Peace-keeping*, United Nations, 31 January, 1992, https://digitallibrary.un.org/record/145749?ln=en&v=pdf.

118 African Union, *Rwanda: The Preventable Genocide*, refworld: Global Law and Policy Database, July, 2000, https://www.refworld.org/reference/countryrep/au/2000/en/77155.

119 International Alert, 'International Alert Statement on Philippines Transition', 13 July, 2023, https://www.international-alert.org/statements/international-alert-statement-on-philippines-transition/.

120 Transforming INGO Models for Equity, *Partnerships and Power: Understanding the Dynamics Between International and National Sexual and Reproductive Health and Rights Organisations*, EngenderHealth and Humentum, April, 2023, https://www.engenderhealth.org/wp-content/uploads/2023/04/Partnerships-and-Power-Understanding-the-Dynamics-Between-SRHR-INGOs-and-NNGOs.pdf.

Chapter 8

121 Nicola Banks, Badru Bukenya, Willem Elbers, et al., *Where Do We Go From Here? Navigating Power Inequalities Between Development NGOs in the Aid System*, Partos, January, 2024, https://globalfundcommunityfoundations.org/wp-content/uploads/2024/01/WhereDoWeGoFromHere_PolicyBrief.pdf.

122 Ennie Chipembere, Kim Kucinskas, and Cynthia Smith, 'Opinion: Equitable Development – Aspiration or Actuality?', Devex, 1 August, 2023, https://www.devex.com/news/sponsored/opinion-equitable-development-aspiration-or-actuality-103123.

123 RINGO Project and West Africa Civil Society Institute, 'Voices from the South, What Can INGOs and Funders do to Shift Power?', West Africa Civil Society Institute,

Summary poster, January, 2024, https://drive.google.com/file/d/109p7ErYNfJXobfQ9HLiBZfMFTO8Hx_Kg/view?usp=sharing.

[124] World Economic Forum, 'Energy Transition: Which Countries are Making the Most Progress in 2023 – and Which Have More Work to Do?', 14 November, 2023, https://www.weforum.org/agenda/2023/10/energy-transition-progress-trilemma/#:~:text=Out%20of%20the%20120%20countries,been%20uneven%2C%20and%20countries%20much.

[125] Climate Council, '11 Countries Leading the Charge on Renewable Energy', 15 August, 2022, https://www.climatecouncil.org.au/11-countries-leading-the-charge-on-renewable-energy/.

[126] Bert Maerten, 'Reflections on HelpAge's Transformation Journey', HelpAge, 11 October, 2023, https://www.stoppingassuccess.org/resources/reflections-on-helpages-transformation-journey/.

[127] Karen Hirschfeld, 'What is a Local Organization? The Answer Matters', Oxfam, 8 January, 2024, https://politicsofpoverty.oxfamamerica.org/what-is-a-local-organization-the-answer-matters/.

[128] Jenny Lei Ravelo, 'The World's Largest NGO Rethinks its Future', Devex, 13 January, 2021, https://www.devex.com/news/the-world-s-largest-ngo-rethinks-its-future-98629.

[129] John Githongo, 'Thirty Years of Anti-Corruption: A Personal Reflection', The Elephant, 23 February, 2024, https://www.theelephant.info/reflections/2024/02/23/thirty-years-of-anti-corruption-a-personal-reflection/.

[130] RINGO Project and West Africa Civil Society Institute, 'Fostering Equitable North–South Civil Society Partnerships', RightsCoLab, March, 2021, https://rightscolab.org/ringo-projects-first-research-report-voices-from-the-south/.

[131] RightsCoLab, *Re-Imagining INGO Prototypes: Summary of the Initial RINGO Prototypes Endorsed by the Ringo Social Lab*, May, 2022, https://rightscolab.org/wp-content/uploads/2022/05/FINAL-RINGO-Prototypes_May22_PUBLIC.pdf.

[132] One World Together, 'Join Our Wave of Change', 2024, https://oneworldtogether.org.uk/join-us/.

[133] Pledge for Change, 'Pledge for Change – Home', n.d., https://pledgeforchange2030.org; Partos, 'Home – Partos', 2024, https://www.partos.nl; International Civil Society Centre, 'The International Civil Society Centre – Helping International Civil Society Organisations (ICSOs) Maximise Their Impact', n.d., https://icscentre.org; NEAR, 'NEAR', n.d., https://www.near.ngo; #ShiftThePower, 'Another Way Is Possible', 2023, https://shiftthepower.org.

134 People of Colour in Development Working Group, 'Three Years On from the Murder of George Floyd: Where Are We Now?', Bond, 23 August, 2023, https://www.bond.org.uk/news/2023/08/three-years-on-from-the-murder-of-george-floyd-where-are-we-now/.

135 E.F. Schumacher, *Small is Beautiful: A Study of Economics as if People Mattered*, London: Abacus, 1975.

136 Hibak Kalfan, speech at Shift the Power Summit, Bogota, 7 December, 2023.

137 Global Fund for Community Foundations, *#ShiftthePower: A Manifesto for Change*, November, 2019, https://www.greengrants.org/wp-content/uploads/2021/04/ShiftthePower-A-Manifesto-for-Change.pdf.

138 Themrise Khan, 'Opinion: Confessions of an Angry Global South Development Practitioner', Devex, 21 July, 2023, https://www.devex.com/news/opinion-confessions-of-an-angry-global-south-development-practitioner-105927?utm_source=linkedin&utm_medium=social&utm_campaign=devex_social_icons.

139 Partos, 'Launch Shift the Power Research – Navigating Power Inequalities between Northern and Southern NGOs', webinar, 11 January, 2024, https://www.youtube.com/watch?v=pAVbUQsoS-c.

140 Peace Direct, 'The Nine Roles that Intermediaries can Play in International Cooperation', 11 January, 2023, https://www.peacedirect.org/the-nine-roles-that-intermediaries-can-play-in-international-cooperation/.

141 Vu Le, 'About', NonProfit AF, April, 2023, https://nonprofitaf.com/about/#:~:text=Vu%20Le%20(%E2%80%9Cvoo%20lay%E2%80%9D,fostering%20collaboration%20among%20diverse%20communities.

Printed in the USA
CPSIA information can be obtained
at www.ICGtesting.com
JSHW011548090924
69567JS00016BA/684